David Young

Historical Facts and Thrilling Incidents of the Niagara Frontier

David Young

Historical Facts and Thrilling Incidents of the Niagara Frontier

ISBN/EAN: 9783742810021

Manufactured in Europe, USA, Canada, Australia, Japa

Cover: Foto ©ninafisch / pixelio.de

Manufactured and distributed by brebook publishing software (www.brebook.com)

David Young

Historical Facts and Thrilling Incidents of the Niagara Frontier

Historical ✻ Facts

—— AND ——

THRILLING INCIDENTS

— OF THE —

NIAGARA FRONTIER

BY

DAVID YOUNG.

NIAGARA FALLS, N. Y.:

Preface.

The Falls of Niagara are among the most wonderful works of nature, and since their first discovery by Father Hennepin in 1678, rich and poor, high and low, kings and plebians, have done homage to this wonder of wonders. All nations of the world have furnished their quota of tourists to this center of attraction. Consequently many stirring events have taken place in this vicinity, which prove the old adage that "Truth is stranger than fiction." The Niagara Frontier is rich in historical facts, many battles having been fought near the boundary line in the early days. The writer, who has lived within the roar of the mighty Cataract for more than half a century, is well acquainted with some of the incidents herein narrated, and the facts contained in this book have been secured from the most authentic sources. The book will be found very valuable to all interested in our Frontier History, and will supply a want long felt by the traveling public.

The Niagara River.

This picturesque river extends from Lake Erie to Lake Ontario, a distance of thirty-six miles, and through it passes all the waters of the great lakes of the west, including Lakes Superior, Michigan, Huron, St. Clair and Erie, forming the largest and finest body of fresh water in the world. It has a fall from Lake Erie to the Falls of 68 feet on the American and 78 on the Canadian side. The American fall is 160 feet high and the Canadian or horse-shoe fall is 150 feet in height. From the base of the falls to Lewiston, a distance of seven miles, there is a fall of 104 feet; and from Lewiston to the mouth of the river at Lake Ontario, a distance of seven miles more, there is a fall of two feet, making a fall of 334 feet from lake to lake.

This river is dotted with numerous beautiful islands, thirty six in all, the largest of which is Grand Island containing about eleven thousand acres of land. But the one which is of the most interest to the tourist is Goat Island, which divides the American from the Canadian or horse-shoe fall, and is now included in the State Reservation.

As the river is the dividing line between the United States and Canada, many stirring scenes have taken place near its shores. Numerous and bloody battles have been fought within its vicinity. For more than a hundred years there was war between France and England, and the contest did not cease until 1763, when French rule in North America was wiped out. So that from the earliest days of the rule of the American aborigines to the close of our own war of 1812, its borders have been the scenes of many conflicts and of deeds of heroism and valor.

The Griffin.

Five miles above the falls, near the mouth of Cayuga Creek, is a village called LaSalle, so named after LaSalle, who, in company with father Hennepin, built the first boat at this place that ever sailed on the great lakes. The boat was called the Griffin and was about sixty tons burden. It was early in the year 1678 that the work of building this vessel began under great difficulties. The savages hovered around the ship builders, and entered the camp with a lack of ceremony rather alarming. They refused to sell their corn, and plotted to burn the vessel on the stocks. Suffering from cold, and often from hunger, fearing always a hostile descent of the savages, the men became discontented, and it required Father Hennepin's utmost endeavors to allay their fears. Meanwhile LaSalle was at Frontenac, whither he had returned after driving the first bolt of the brigantine, endeavoring to counteract the efforts of his enemies who were spreading reports that he was about to engage in an extremely dangerous undertaking, enormously expensive and yielding but little hope of his return. Their rumors so alarmed his creditors in Quebec and

Montreal that they seized upon his effects there and sold them out at great loss to him. The delay which would be necessary to rectify this would prevent the success of his expedition, for this year at least, so he submitted patiently to his misfortunes.

At last the ship was ready and his other preparations were complete. On the seventh day of August, 1679, the sails of the Griffin were spread to the winds of Lake Erie, and making fearlessly for the midst of the great fresh water sea, they descried, on the third day the islands in the western end. A storm beset them in Huron, and with the usual bitterness of the followers of great explorers, many of his men complained of the dangers into which they had been led. They escaped from the storm, however, but only to meet with new difficulties. Their first object was to make a favorable impression upon the Indians, whose friendship was so necessary to their success; but this task was harder than they had anticipated. While the natives received and entertained LaSalle with great civility and looked in wonder at the great wooden canoe, their show of friendship was more politic than sincere, and produced no effect upon their future conduct. Nor was this the only disadvantage under which they labored. Fifteen men had been sent forward to collect provisions, but had been tampered with, and had squandered a part of the merchandise with which they had been provided for trading. However, hoping that some would prove faithful to their trust, a belief which later events justified, they continued on their course.

On his way across the lakes, LaSalle marked Detroit as a suitable place for a colony, gave name to Lake St. Clair, planted a trading house at Mackinaw, and finally cast anchor at Green Bay. Here, to retrieve his fortune, he collected a rich cargo of furs, and sent back his brig to carry them to Niagara. But unfortunately, the brig, with the cargo, was lost on her way down the lakes, and no reliable information was ever obtained of her fate.

The old Stone Chimney.

On the American side of the river, about one and a half miles above the falls, there is still standing an old chimney as a relic of scenes of strife in days that are past and gone. This chimney stands on land now owned by the Cataract Construction Company and within a quarter of a mile of the power house of the great tunnel. We understand they intend to preserve it. It was built by the French in 1750. And close by are still marks of old Fort Schlosser, which was then called Fort DuPortage. All of which was destroyed by fire in 1759, the French making their escape into Canada when being threatened with an attack by the British under Sir Wm. Johnson who had just captured Fort Niagara. But this chimney was so substantially constructed that it passed through the fire unharmed. Soon after this the fort and barracks were rebuilt by the English troops under command of Captain Joseph Schlosser, a German who served in the

British army and was afterwards promoted to the rank of colonel, and died in the Fort. An oak slab on which his name was cut was standing at his grave just above the fort as late as the year 1808. On the west side of the aforesaid chimney are still standing some of the surviving trees of the first apple orchard set out in this region, and as early as 1796 it was described as being a well fenced orchard, containing 1200 trees, only a few of which are now remaining. The building which was erected by the English to the old chimney was afterwards used as a dwelling house by different persons, among whom was the late Judge Porter, who occupied it in the years of 1806,-7-8, when he removed to the Porter homestead on Buffalo street. This building was afterwards converted into a tavern for the accommodation of visitors to the Falls and travelers en route to the west, and was so occupied when again destroyed in 1813 by the British who made a raid on this side of the river. Some of the inmates made their escape by hiding in a deep ditch running through a large meadow on the east side of the house, and others, thinking to make their escape by way of the orchard on the west side, were met by the Indians, who lay in ambush, and were either killed or taken prisoner.

Afterwards another building was put to the old chimney which was used for a farm house for many years, in which the writer had the pleasure of eating some good meals that were cooked in the fire place of the "Old Stone Chimney," which has withstood the storms of nearly 150 years and passed through a fiery ordeal at three different times.

The Hon. T. V. Welch, who has taken a deep interest in our frontier history, has composed the following verses:

Beside Niagara's lovely stream
  An old stone chimney stands,
In winter's blast, and summer's beam,
  Above the river sands;
Oft on the hearth in childhood's day,
  A glowing fire was made,
And in the summer gray,
  'Round the old stone chimney played.

CHORUS:—

Touch not the old stone chimney;
  Our grandsire's long ago,
Their youthful bride's beside that hearth,
  Loved in the cheerful glow;
Touch not the old stone chimney,
  Where the red man used to dwell,
Where the pioneer and his sweetheart dear,
  They sleep, they sleep, so well.

The fire-light fell, on the children there,
  And youth dreamt in its blaze;
And gentle wives, and daughters fair,
  Sweethearts of other days;
Oft since that day, has love held sway,
  And plighted hearts and hands;
Beside Niagara's winding way,
  Where the old stone chimney stands.

                CHORUS.

Long may the old stone chimney stand
  Upon Niagara's shore;
The sons of France, and Britain's band,
  They battle there no more;
The pioneer and sweetheart's dear,
  Are sleeping on the hill,
Where lone the old stone chimney stands,
  In the evening gray and still.

                CHORUS.

The Campaign of 1759.

It is not the intention to give a complete history of the French and English war, but simply so much of it as is of local interest and some of the results. The campaign of 1759 had for its object the entire reduction of Canada. After the disaster of Ticonderoga, the chief command of the British forces was given to Gen. Amherst. The army was divided into three parts, exhibiting the following order: The first division, under Wolf, was to make a direct attempt upon Quebec. The second, under Amherst, was ordered to take Ticonderoga and Crown Point, and then proceed northerly; and the third, under Gen. Prideaux, consisting of provincials and Indians, was to reduce Niagara, then to go down the St. Lawrence, and, jointly with the second detachment, attack Montreal. Thus the several detachments were to enter Canada by different routes, but were all destined, eventually, to meet before Quebec, and it was against that keystone of the arch, which sustained the French power in America, that that the grand final effort was to be made.

Prideaux besieged Niagara on the 1st of July. He was killed on the 15th by the bursting of a 24-pound brass mortar and the command devolved upon Sir. William Johnson. The French and Indians, numbering about 1200, came to the relief of the garrison and gave battle to the English, but the Indians in their alliance deserted them in the heat of the engagement, and victory was declared in favor of the English. On the 25th of July the garrison consisting of 600 men, fell into the hands of the British, who now possessed this important post, barring all communications between the northern and southern possessions of the French. We can not give a narrative of all of the different battles in this campaign, which were truly important, but simply say that this war did not cease until the treaty of peace was declared in Paris on February 10th, 1763, when England got undisputed possession (except by the Indians) of the whole continent, from the shores of the Gulf of Mexico to the frozen north, and from ocean to ocean.

Indian Strategy.

In 1763, Pontiac, a sagacious Ottawa chief, and a former ally of the French, thought that if the English could be subdued before they could gain a firm foot-hold, the Indians would again be lords of the forest. For this purpose he secretly effected a confederation of several of the north-western tribes of Indians, and on the 7th of July nine of the British forts were captured by them, which were all of the forts west of Oswego, excepting Fort Niagara, Fort Pitt and Detroit. Pontiac had arranged the following plans of strategy: At Maumee, the commanding officer was lured forth by piteous entreaties of a squaw, who feigned to plead for a wounded man dying without the fort, and he was immediately shot by Indians in ambush.

At Mackinaw, a more important post, the Indians had gathered by hundreds. They began among themselves a spirited game of ball. One of the two parties who played, drove the other, as if by accident, towards the palisades which inclosed the grounds of the fort. They came on, shouting and sporting, and the soldiers went forth to view the game. At length the ball was thrown over the pickets, and the Indians jumped after it within the inclosure. Then began the butchery. The soldiers of the garrison, appalled and unprepared, could make no resistance. The commander, Major Henry, was writing within his room. He heard the Indian war-cry, and the shrieks of the murdered; and from the window he saw four-hundred savages cutting down with their tomahawks, his dearest friends. He saw them scalped while yet in their death struggles, their necks beneath their feet, or their heads held between the knees of the scalpers. They had already taken the fort, but Henry himself, through some strange perils, escaped to relate the horrible scene.

Pontiac chose to command in person at Detroit, that post being regarded as the key to the upper country. On the 6th, the Indians, to the number of six hundred, had collected in the woods around the fort. In the evening a squaw who had been kindly treated, betrayed to Major Gladwyn, the commander, the designs of the savages. On the 7th, Pontiac, with a party of his chiefs, presented themselves as in peace, desiring to hold a council with the officers within the fort. They were admitted, but to their surprise, they were immediately surrounded by the garrison, fully armed. Major Gladwyn approached Pontiac, and lifting his blanket found a short rifle concealed beneath it. Thus unexpectedly discovered, Pontiac himself was disconcerted. The Indians from without were not let in; but the chief escaped, or was suffered to go forth.

He then beseiged the fort, holding the garrison confined for many months, and cutting off supplies and reinforcements. At length his allies grew weary of war, and peace was declared. Pontiac died three years afterwards.

Devil's Hole Massacre.

The Devil's Hole is a picturesque place on the American side, about a mile below the Whirlpool. It is here where on the 14th of September, 1763, the Seneca Indians, smarting under English rule, lay in ambush for a British supply train on its way from Schlosser to Lewiston. And as the doomed company carelessly filed along the brink of the chasm, a murderous volley was fired by the hidden savages, who then sprang forth thirty or forty to one of the survivors, and butchered them with tomahawk and scalping knife. Crazed by the din of firearms and the yells of the savages, part of the teams went off the rocky wall; and even the men in some cases, rather than be hacked to pieces on the spot or roasted at the stake, flung themselves from the cliff. Among the latter was a drummer boy named Mathews, who fell into a tree top, from which he descended without mortal injuries. It is said that only three survived this savage onset. John Steadman, who commanded the supply train, seeing the fatal snare at the first fire of the Indians, spurred his horse through the leaden hail and made his escape, reaching Fort Schlosser in safety. A wounded soldier concealed himself in the dense evergreen bushes and thus escaped the knife and the hatchet; and the drummer boy who was saved by lodging in the tree top. These were the only ones left to tell the sad tale.

The firing had been heard by the guard posted at the lower landing, and suspecting the state of the case they hastened up the Portage Road. The savages had time to complete the destruction of the train and its escort and ensconce themselves again in the bushes, with rifles reloaded and tomahawks all ready, before the reinforcements reached the spot, when the massacre was renewed. A shower of bullets from the thicket tore through the close lines of the detachment, felling more than one half of the troops; again the thirsty savages, sallying from their cover, swarmed around their prey, and the scalping knives yet dripping with blood from their latest use, were bathed anew in human gore. Only eight men escaped with their lives, who bore the horrible tidings to Fort Niagara. The number of killed is variously estimated as being from 80 to 250.

The little rivulet falling into the glen, and called Bloody Run, first became such on that dreadful day when its waters were crimsoned by the butchery upon its banks. The passerby now looks from his carriage down the gloomy pit, which yawns close beside the roadway, into the bristling treetops that hide its lowest depths, and shudder to think of the situation of the men who judged it best to cast themselves into this deep and rugged chasm. Yet one who made this choice long outlived every other actor in this awful tragedy—the drummer Mathews—who died in Queenston at the advanced age of 90 years.

Tuscarora Reservation.

About seven miles northeast of Niagara Falls, is situated the Tuscarora Indian Reservation. History tells us that in 1712 the Tuscaroras and other Indians from North Carolina, formed, with all the subtlety of the savage character, a plot for exterminating the entire white population. Having kept their design a profound secret until the night fixed for its execution, they entered the houses of the poor Palatines of Germany who had settled on the Roanoke and murdered men, women and children. A few who escaped gave the alarm and the remaining inhabitants, collecting into camp, kept guard night and day until aid could be received from South Carolina. That colony sent to their relief 600 militia and 360 Indians under Barnwell. Although a wilderness at this time separated the northern from the southern settlements, Barnwell penetrated it, boldly attacked the Indians, killed 300 and took 100 prisoners. Those who escaped fled to the chief town of the Tuscaroras, where they erected wooden breastworks for their security; but here Barnwell's troops surrounded them and they at last sued for peace. The Tuscaroras had lost a thousand men in the course of this war and they soon after left their country and settled in Central New York, uniting with the Iroquois, making the sixth nation of that confederacy. During the struggle for American independence part of this tribe joined the British forces and part maintained a strict neutrality. Such of the Tuscaroras and Oneidas as had allied themselves with the English and fled before the arrival of Sullivan's army sought refuge within the British garrison at Fort Niagara, reaching there via the Oneida Lake, Oswego Lake and Lake Ontario. During the early part of the following year part of them returned to their hunting-grounds in Central New York and part of them took possession of a mile square on the mountain range, which was given to them by the Senecas who owned the territory there. At a later period the Holland Land Co. granted them two square miles adjoining their possessions and in 1808 they purchased of the company an additional tract, making, in the aggregate, 7,620 acres now in their possession. The reservation has the appearance of any other agricultural neighborhood. The present population is about 460, few, if any, looking like the "red man of the forest" of whom we use to read in our schoolboy days. They have two churches—Presbyterian and Baptist, and the community is a well behaved one with few exceptions. The Indian children now receive school training, and many of them show a marked degree of intelligence, and an aptitude for learning. There is considerable musical talent among these Indians and the Tuscarora Band has played in some of the principal cities of our country in connection with a show of "Indian Beauties," among whom were some Tuscarora maidens.

The War of 1812.

The reasons for the war with England, as stated by Mr. Madison, President of the United States, in an able manifesto, were: British excesses in violating the American flag on the great highway of nations; the impressment of American seamen; harrassing American vessels as they were entering their own harbors or departing from them, and wantonly spilling the blood of the citizens of America within the limits of her territorial jurisdiction; issuing orders by which the ports of the enemies of Great Britain were blockaded, and not supporting these blockades by the adequate application of fleets to render them legal, and enforcing them from the date of their proclamation, in consequence of which American commerce had been plundered on every sea, and her products cut off from their legitimate market: employing secret agents to subvert the government and dismember the Union; and finally encouraging the Indian tribes to hostility. Still the American people long cherished the hope that a sense of justice would induce the British Ministry to bring to a speedy and honorable termination the unfortunate differences subsisting between the two nations. They were unwilling to resort to the ultimate means of redress until all peaceful measures had been exhausted, and, indeed, so tardy was the government in its preparations for war, that the people in many parts of the country loudly complained of its want of firmness and energy. But delay brought no redress. Injury was followed by indignity, until the peaceful policy of the Government at length yielded, and on the 18th of June, 1812, war was formally declared against Great Britain and its dependencies, by the Congress of the United States.

The Surrender of Hull.

Previous to the declaration of war, Gen. Hull, in anticipation of that event, had been appointed to the command of a large and well furnished army, intended for the invasion of Canada from some point near Detroit. This army passed Cincinnati the latter part of May, left Dayton on the 1st of June, arrived on the Maumee River on the 30th and crossed the River of Detroit—for the invasion of Canada—on the 12th of July. The expedition was attended with the high hopes of the people, the officers and the men. It was opposed by no superior force, and when in front of the enemy no sound of discontent was heard, nor any appearance of cowardice or dissatisfaction seen. On the contrary every man awaited the battle in sure anticipation of victory, expecting a proud day for his country and himself. Notwithstanding all this preparation, notwithstanding the superiority of the force, and notwithstanding these vivid anticipations of success and glory, the entire army was, without apparent cause, surrendered to the demand of General Brock, on the 14th day of August.

This event, so unexpected and so disastrous, filled the American people with consternation and mortification. Indignation, grief and shame alternately filled the hearts of the honest citizen and the patriot soldier. It was a veil of darkness drawn over the face of the country.

Such was the commencement of the war of 1812, unfortunate, disastrous and melancholy. It was certainly no encouragement to those who soon after commenced the campaign of the Niagara, where bloody fields, brave actions and positive achievements, reanimated the hopes of the country, and gave a durable glory to the American arms.

———◆———

A Naval Engagement.

In July 1812 Winfield Scott received the commission of Lieutenant-Colonel in the 2d artillery, (Izard's regiment), and arrived on the Niagara frontier, with companies of Towson and Barker. He took post at Black Rock to protect the navy yard there established.

Lieutenant Elliott of the navy had planned an enterprise against two armed brigs, then lying at anchor under the guns of Fort Erie. For this purpose he applied on the 8th of August, 1812, to Colonel Scott for assistance in officers and men. Captain Towson and a portion of his company were dispatched to the aid of Elliott. The attack was successful. On the morning of the ninth, both vessels were carried in the most gallant manner. The "Adams" was taken by Captain Elliott in person, assisted by Lieutenant Isaac Roach; and the "Caledonia" by the gallant Captain Towson. In dropping down the Niagara River the "Adams" became unmanagable through the occurrence of a calm, and drifted into the British channel. She got aground on Squaw Island, directly under the guns of the enemy's batteries, where it was impossible to get her off. Captain Elliott, therefore, having previously secured the prisoners, abandoned her under a heavy fire from the British shore. Then ensued an interesting and exciting scene, the British endeavoring to retake the abandoned brig and Scott to prevent them. The enemy sent out boats, and Scott resisted them, in which effort he was successful. The brig was recaptured and held until she was subsequently burned by order of General Smythe, who had then arrived.

As for the "Caledonia" she was preserved by the extraordinary efforts of Captain Towson, and afterwards did good service in the memorable and glorious victory won on Lake Erie, by the gallant Perry.

Although this was not so important an engagement as the capture of the British frigate Guerriere, under command of Captain Dacres, by the American frigate Constitution, commanded by Captain Hull, which took place off the Grand Bank of Newfoundland, a few days after the disgraceful surrender of Detroit, yet this was one of those small but honorable enterprises, of which many occurred during the war, which should be mentioned to the credit of the actors, and as an example to those who hereafter may have similiar duties to perform in defence of their country.

The Battle of Queenston Heights.

In the beginning of October, 1812, Major-General Stephen Van Rensselaer had collected together, at Lewiston, about two thousand five hundred of the New York Militia. The successful enterprise which resulted in the capture of the "Adams" and "Caledonia" on the 9th of that month, had given such an apparent ardor and impulse to these troops that it was believed impossible to restrain them. Indeed, the troops declared they must act, or go home, an alternative which imposed upon the General the necessity of some active movement. Accordingly, he planned an attack on Queenston Heights. The troops which he had at his command were the New York militia and about four hundred and fifty regulars under the command of Colonels Fenwick and Chrystie, who, with Major Mullaney, had arrive the night before in detachments from Fort Niagara for the purpose of joining in this expedition. The militia were raw, inexperienced, and undisciplined, circumstances which caused the brunt of the battle ultimately to fall on the regulars, and its final loss.

The plan was to throw over the river two columns of troops, each about three hundred strong. One was commanded by Colonel Solomon Van Rensselaer, and the other by Lieutenant-Colonel Chrystie The detachments of Fenwick and Mullaney were to sustain, in the best way they could, these columns. These arrangements were made on the 12th of October. Late in the evening of that day Col. Scott had arrived by a forced march, partly by water and partly through mud and rain, at Schlosser, two miles above the Falls and nine from Lewiston, with a view of joining in the contemplated attack. He hastened to Lewiston and volunteered his services to General Van Rensselaer. They were declined on account of the arrangements already made; but with permission that Scott should bring his regiment immediately to Lewiston, and there act as circumstances might require, and opportunities offer. This permission he at once availed himself of, and arrived at Lewiston with his corps at four o'clock a. m. on the 13th. Finding no boats he placed his train in battery on the American shore under the immediate command of Captains Towson and Barker, and when daylight appeared opened an effective fire on the enemy.

In the meantime the principal movement, as originally planned, had gone on. All the boats which could be collected were employed to transport the columns of Chrystie and Van Rensselaer. Unfortunately the boats were insufficient to take the whole number at once, and the passage was made by detachments. The boat in which Chrystie was became disabled, was mismanaged by the pilot, and finally carried out of the way by the eddies of the river. He made a gallant attempt to land but was wounded and had to return to the American shore. In the after part of the engagement he returned with reinforcements to the troops in Canada and shared the fate of the day.

The main body of the first embarkation, under the direction of Colonel Van Rensselaer, was more successful.

Two companies of the 13th Regiment, with other small detachments of the same regiment, were able to land, and were successively reinforced from time to time as the few servicible boats to be had could transport them. They were landed under a severe fire of the enemy. At this time the numbers of both contending parties were small. The British force was composed of two flank companies of the 49th and the York militia. The Americans did not number much over one hundred combatants. Notwithstanding the continued cannonade from the enemies batteries this small force formed on the bank and marched steadily forward.

In a few moments this fire had killed or wounded every commissioned officer, and among these Colonel Van Rensselaer himself, who received four severe wounds. Notwithstanding this, he sustained himself long enough to impart the local information he possessed to other officers, who had in the meantime come up. In leaving the field his last command was that "all such as could move should immediately mount the hill and storm the batteries." This order was promptly obeyed by Captain Wool, on whom, as then senior officer of the regular troops, the command devolved, and he was also bleeding from his wounds, but distinguished himself with Captains Ogilvie, Malcolm and Armstrong and Lieutenant Randolph. These brave officers stormed the heights, took a battery composed of an eighteen-pounder and two mortars half way up the declivity, and were soon in possession of the highest point, called the "mountain." By this time the enemy were beaten, routed, and driven into a strong stone building near the water's edge.

Elated with their success, the Americans had fallen into disorder, when they again beheld 300 of their foe, advancing under the intrepid Brock, the lieutenant-governor of Upper Canada, who had just returned from the capture of Hull to defend the Niagara frontier. An officer raised a white flag in token to surrender; Wool indignantly pulled it down. The British now drove the Americans to the edge of the incline. One soldier was about to descend; Wool ordered him to be shot; but, as the musket was leveled, he returned. Thus prohibiting either surrender or retreat, and being ably seconded by his officers, he rallied and led on his troops to the attack. The British in their turn gave way, and retreated down the hill. Brock, while attempting to rally them in the midst of a galling fire, was mortally wounded. His party no longer attempted resistance, but fled in disorder.

Exactly at this period Lieutenant-colonel Scott arrived on the heights He had been permitted, as a volunteer, to cross the river with his adjutant, Roach, and assume the command of the whole body engaged. On the Canada side he unexpectedly found Brigadier-General William Wadsworth of the New York militia, who had crossed without orders Scott therefore proposed to limit his command to the regulars, but the generous and patriotic Wadsworth would not consent. Scott then assumed command, and throughout the movements that ensued General Wadsworth dared every danger in aiding the views of the commander. Reinforcements having arrived during the previous engagements, the troops under Scott now amounted in all to three hundred and fifty regulars, and two hundred and fifty volunteers, under the direction of General Wadsworth and Colonel Stranahan. These Scott, upon the suggestion of Captain Tatton, drew up in a strong and commanding situation. The object in view was not only to receive the enemy, but to cover the ferry in expectation of being reinforced by the whole of the militia at Lewiston.

The interval of rest was short. The first gun which broke the silence of the morning had also aroused the British garrison of Fort George eight miles below. Their troops were instantly put in motion. The Indians, who had been concentrated in the vicinity, sprang into activity. In a short time five hundred of these forest warriors joined the British light companies previously engaged. A new battle ensued. The Americans received the enemy with firmness and drove them back in total route.

The protection of the ferry being the main purpose, and as the Indians in the wood presented no opportunity for a charge, the Americans resumed their original position, and there maintained it valiantly against several successive attacks, until the British reinforcements arrived from Fort George. In one of these affairs the advanced pickets of the American lines were suddenly driven in by superior numbers, and a general massacre seemed inevitable. At this critical moment Scott, who had been in the rear showing how to unspike a captured cannon, hastily returned and by great exertions brought his line, then in the act of giving away, to the right-about. His brilliant example produced a sudden revulsion of feeling. They caught the spirit of their leader. With an unanimous burst of enthusiasm the line suddenly rallied from right to left, threw itself forward upon the enemy, putting him to a precipitate flight, and strewing the ground with the dead and wounded. In this manner successive conflicts were kept up till the main body of the British reinforcements arrived. This was a column eight hundred and fifty strong under the command of Major-General Sheaffe, who was afterwards made a baronet for the events of the day.

During the action, which had now so long proceeded with credit to the American troops, the Militia who had crossed the river and were engaged with Wadsworth and Stranahan, had fought well, and shared both the dangers and the successes of the day. At this crisis, however, when the result of the battle depended entirely upon reinforcements, information was brought to Scott and those engaged that the Militia on the American shore refused to cross. General Van Rensselaer rode among them in all directions, urging the men by every consideration to pass, but in vain. Not a regiment nor a company could be induced to move. A panic had seized them; but even had it been otherwise they could not have crossed, as but a few crippled boats remained to take them over. The total number of boats in the beginning was only thirteen. Severe was the mortification of this disaster to the brave men engaged, and mournful the result.

At this period the British was estimated, regulars, militia and Indians, at not less than thirteen hundred, while the Americans were reduced to less than three hundred. Retreat was as hopeless as success; for there were no boats on the Canadian shore, and the militia on the other side refused to give them aid. Scott took his position on the grounds they then occupied, resolved to abide the shock, and think of surrender only when battle was impossible. He mounted a log in front of his much-diminished band. "The enemy's balls," said he, "begin to thin our ranks. His numbers are overwhelming. In a moment the shock must come. We are in the beginning of a national war. Hull's surrender is to be redeemed. Let us then die arms in hand. Our country demands the sacrifice. The example will not be lost. The blood of the slain will make heroes of the living. Those who follow will avenge our fall and their country's wrongs. Who dare to stand?" "All!" was the answering cry. In the meanwhile the British, under the command of Major-General Sheaffe, manoeuvred with great caution, and even hesitation, conscious of the vigorous resistance already made, and determined fully to reconnoiter. They found it difficult to believe that so small a body of men was the whole force they had to contend with, and supposed it rather an outpost than an army. At length the attack began. The Americans for a time maintained their resolution, but finally began to give way. When nearly surrounded they let themselves (by holding on limbs and bushes) down the precipice to the river. Resistance was now ended and after a brief consultation it was determined to send a flag to the enemy, with a proposition to capitulate. Several persons were successively sent, but neither answer nor messenger returned; they were all shot down or captured by the Indians. At length Scott determined that he himself would make another attempt. He prepared a flag of truce—a white handkerchief fastened upon his sword—and accompanied by Captains Totton and Gibson went forth on a forlorn hope to seek a parley. Keeping close to the water's edge and under cover of the precipice as much as possible, they descended along the river. They were exposed to a continual random fire from the Indians, until they turned up an easy slope to gain the road from the village to the heights. They had just attained this road when they were met by two Indians, who sprang upon them. It was in vain that Scott declared his purpose and claimed the protection of his flag. They attempted to wrench it from his hands, and at the same instant Totton and Gibson drew their swords. The Indians had just discharged their rifles at the American officers and were on the point of using their knives and hatchets, when a British officer, accompanied by some men, rushed forward and prevented a further combat.

The three American officers were conducted into the presence of General Sheaffe; terms of capitulation were agreed upon; and Scott surrendered his whole force with the honors of war. The entire force thus surrendered, of those who had been actually fighting, were 139 regulars and 154 militia, making in all 293. But to the intense mortification of Scott, the number was soon swelled by several hundreds of militia, who had crossed to the Canada shore, and in the confusion of the moment, had concealed themselves under the rocks higher up the river, and were not in the slightest degree engaged in the action of the day.

The total loss of the Americans in this battle was estimated at 1000 men. About 100 were killed, 200 who had landed with Major Mullaney early in the day were forced by the current of the river on the enemy's shores under his batteries and were there captured. 293 surrendered with Scott, and the remainder were those who had landed, but were not in the battle.

Thus ended the battle of Queenston Heights; an engagement desultory in its movements, various in its incidents, and unfortunate in its result; but not without consequent importance to the spirit and vigor of the American arms. Magnitude is not always necessary to the dignity of an achievement, nor is defeat always discouraging to the unsuccessful party. It is the nature of the action which gives character to the actor. Judged by this standard, the events of Queenston had their value, and their inspiration to every patriot American. Hull had surrendered without a battle; disgrace, not from the mere disaster, but from the mode by which it was produced was inflicted upon the country, and felt in the hearts of its children. It was battle, and honorable battle only, which could drive this gloomy shadow from the country, check the taunts of the enemies, remove its own doubts, and re-establsh its self respect. The battle of Queenston Heights did this in no small degree. While the mistakes, the errors, and the losses of the day were deplored, the American press and people recognized, amid regrets and misfortune, a spirit of achievement, a boldness in danger, and a gallant bearing, which inspired new hopes, and pointed out the way to ultimate success. The daring gallantry of Colonel Van Rensselaer; the capture of the British battery by Wool and his heroic companions; the intrepid conduct of Wadsworth, of Chrystie, of Totton, and Scott, and many others, had given a cheerfulness even to the darkness of defeat, and almost a glow of satisfaction to the memory of Queenston Heights.

Soon after the surrender, the gallant Brock was buried under one of the bastons of Fort St. George, with the highest of military honors. Fort Niagara, directly opposite on the American shore was commanded at that time by Captain McKeon. Colonel Scott sent over his compliments, and desired that minute-guns might be fired during the funeral ceremonies. Captain McKeon readily complied with the request, for the noble qualities of Brock had been held in equal esteem on both sides of the line It is one of the privileges which smooth the rough brow of war, thus to render a just respect to the worthy dead, whether they be of friends or adversaries. It is the right of magnanimity to carry no hostility beneath the green covering of the grave, nor beyond that line which peace has drawn between noble spirits, that once were foes, nor against those generous qualities which dignify the man and adore the races.

In later years the monument was erected in honor of General Brock which now towers from the top of the Queenston Heights. From this eminent point it can be seen for miles around. The exact spot where Brock fell, near the foot of the hill, has also been appropriately marked, and the place enclosed with a small fence.

Capture of Fort George.

The campaign of 1813 opened with one of the most brilliant actions of the war. It was the capture of York, (now Toronto) the capital of Upper Canada, by the American troops under the command of General Dearborn. The army was landed from the squadron of Commodore Chauncey, and the assisting party was led by Pike. The place was captured, with a large number of prisoners, and the British naval material, there collected, destroyed. At the moment of success a magazine exploded and Pike was killed by the fall of a stone. In a letter written to his father the day before the battle, in speaking of his expedition he was about to engage in, he said: "Should I be the happy mortal destined to turn the scale of war, will you not rejoice, oh my father? May heaven be propitious, and smile on the cause of my country. But if we are destined to fall, may my fall be like Wolf's—to sleep in the arms of victory." The wish was fulfilled. He died like Wolf, in the arms of victory, and the tears of grief and joy were mingled together at the story of the battle which was won, and of the hero who died.

On the British side of the Niagara was Fort George. This position, soon after the last event, General Dearborn determined to carry. He was then at the head of four or five thousand men, and was co-operated with by Commodore Chauncey and his naval force. Arrangements were made for an attack on the morning of the 27th of May. At 3 A. M. the fleet weighed anchor, and before four the troops were all on board the boats. The embarkation was made about three miles east of Fort Niagara. It was made in six divisions of boats. In the first was Colonel Scott, who led the advanced guard, or forlorn hope, a service to which he had specially volunteered. In the second was Colonel Moses Porter with the field train. Then followed the brigades of Generals Boyd, Winder, Chandler. and a reserve under Colonel A. Macomb. In the meantime Commodore Chauncey had directed his schooners to anchor close in shore, so near as to cover the landing of the troops, and scour by their fire the woods and plain wherever the enemy might make his appearance. Captain Perry, from Erie, had joined Commodore Chauncey on the evening of the 25th, and gallantly volunteered his services in superintending the debarkation of the troops. It was a difficult operation, in consequence of the wind, the current, a heavy surf, and the early commenced fire of the enemy. He was present wherever he could be useful, under showers of musketry. He accompanied the advanced guard through the surf, and rendered special services of which mention has since been made in the highest terms of commendation. It was the budding forth of that professional skill, and that brave and generous conduct, which soon bloomed out in the glory which surrounds the name of the hero of Lake Erie. The landing of Col. Scott was effected on the British shore of Lake Ontario, at nine o'clock in the morning, in good order, at half a mile from the village of Newark, now Niagara-on-the-Lake, and the same distance west of the mouth of the river. He formed his line on the beach, covered by an irregular bank, which served as a partial shield against the enemy's fire. This bank, which was from seven to twelve feet in height, he had to scale against the bayonets of the enemy, who had drawn up his forces, some fifteen hundred men, immediately on its brow. In the first attempt to ascend, the enemy pushed back the assailants. General Dearborn, who was still in the Commodore's ship, seeing with his glass Scott fall backward upon the beach exclaimed, "He is lost! He is killed!" Scott's fall was, however, only momentary. Recovering himself and rallying his men, he reascended the bank, knocking aside the enemy's bayonets, and took a position at the edge of a ravine, a little way in advance. A sharp action of about twenty minutes in length ensued. It was short and desperate, ending in the total rout of the enemy at every point.

Meanwhile Porter with his artillery, and Boyd with a part of his brigade, had landed in the rear of the advance guard, and slightly participated in the close of the action. Scott pursued the rout as far as the village, where he was joined by the 6th regiment of infantry, under the command of Colonel James Miller. As the column was passing Fort Niagara in pursuit, Scott learned from some prisoners caught running out, that the garrison was about to abandon and blow up the place. Two companies were instantly dispatched from the head of the column to save the work, its guns and stores. At the distance of some eighty paces from the fort, one of its magazines exploded. Scott was struck with a piece of timber, thrown from his horse and severely hurt. He nevertheless caused the gate to be forced, and was the first to enter, and tore down the British flag, then waving over the works Being reminded by his prisoners of the danger he incurred from explosion, he directed Captains Hindman and Stockton to snatch away the matches which had been applied by the retreating garrison to two other small magazines. The Fort had been rendered untenable by the American batteries on the opposite shore, and its capture was but the work of a few minutes. This accomplished Scott remounted and was soon at the head of his column, in hot pursuit. This pursuit was continued for five miles, until at length he was recalled by General Boyd in person He had already disregarded two successive orders to the same effect sent by General Lewis, saying to the aids-de-camp who came to him (one of them Lieutenant Worth and the other Major Vandeventer) "Your General does not know that I have the enemy within my power; in seventy minutes I shall capture his whole force. In point of fact, Scott was already in the midst of the British stragglers, with their main body in sight. He would not have been overtaken by Boyd, but that he had waited fifteen minutes for Colonel Burns, his senior officer, who had consented to serve under him. This last Colonel had just crossed the river from the Five-Mile Meadow, in rear of the main body of the enemy, with one troop of cavalry and was then waiting the landing of another now more than half way over. This force constituted the precise additional force which was wanted by Scott to make good the assurance he had sent to General Lewis. With the recall of Scott from the pursuit of the enemy ended the battle and capture of Fort George. The American loss was less than that of the British, and one of the objects set forth in the plan of the campaign was decidedly accomplished.

According to General Dearborn's letter to the Secretary of War, the American loss was 17 killed and 45 wounded; British loss, 90 killed, 160 wounded and 100 prisoners.

This engagement was not without some incidents, one of which may not be out of place to relate. After the capture of Scott, the year before, at Queenston, he was supping with General Sheaffe, and a number of British officers, when one of them, a Colonel, asked him if he had ever seen the neighboring Falls. Scott replied, "Yes, from the American side." To this the other sarcastically replied, "You must have the glory of a successful fight before you can view the cataract in all its grandeur," meaning from the Canadian shore. Scott rejoined, "If it be your intention to insult me, sir, honor should have prompted you first to return me my sword!" General Sheaffe promptly rebuked the British Colonel, and the matter was dropped. At the battle of Fort George among the earliest prisoners taken by the Americans was the same British Colonel, badly wounded. Scott politely borrowed the prisoner's horse, not being able to bring his own in the boats, and gave orders that the prisoner should be treated with all possible attention and kindness. That evening, after the pursuit, and as often as subsequent events permitted, Scott called on the British Colonel. He returned him the horse, and carefully provided for all his wants. Indeed, he obtained permission for him to return to England on his parole, at a time when the belligerents had begun to refuse such favors, as well as all exchanges. At the first of these visits the prisoner delicately remarked, "I have long owed you an apology, sir. You have overwhelmed me with kindness. You can now at your leisure, view the Falls in all their glory."

It is such acts of magnanimity as these which reflect honor on human nature. Were they more frequent, the rough brow of war would be smoothed to smiles, and the field of battle be as remarkable for the beautiful in character as for the glorious in action.

Battle of Stony Creek.

To the successful actions of York, Fort George, and of Sackett's Harbor, there were soon added others of a less fortunate result, and of a less pleasant hue. On the 6th of June a small brigade of about 800 American troops under the command of General Winder, had been thrown forward to Stony Creek, and there reinforced by another corps under Chandler. Their object was the pursuit and capture of the British corps who had retreated from Fort George, under the command of Vincent. This officer thought it better to risk a battle than to give up his position. He prepared also to make the attack. Accordingly on the morning of the 6th, by night, a British column was pushed into the centre of the American line, which Vincent had discovered to be weakened by extension, and liable to surprise, by the negligence of camp guards. The attack succeeded so far as to break the American line, and by a strange misfortune both of the American generals, Winder and Chandler, fell into the hands of the British. When the attack was a made a scene of confusion and carnage ensued, in which the Americans could not distinguish friend from foe. General Chandler approached to rally a party but they proved to be British troops, who immediately secured him as their prisoner. General Winder shared by a like mistake a similiar fate. The Americans, however, maintained their post, and forced the enemy to re-retire, but the army, being without an experienced commander, retreated by the advice of a council of war. The loss of the British exceeded that of the Americans, and was more than one hundred.

A few days after the battle of Stony Creek, another incident still more disastrous occurred On the 24th of June Boerstler had been detached, with a corps of 600 men, to take the British post called Stone House, two miles beyond the Beaver Dams, and 17 miles from Fort George. The British force was larger than was supposed. Boerstler was suffered to advance without annoyance, till at length he was surrounded and compelled to surrender.

The principal reason given for the success of the British on this occasion is found in the following narrative, as related by Mrs. J. J. Currie of St. Catharines, and revised by J. B. Secord of Niagara-on-the-Lake.

Looking from the right hand side of the Niagara Central train about five miles above St. Catharines, the passenger will observe a small obelisk. This stone was erected to mark the spot where on the 24th of June, 1813, took place what is now known as the Battle of the Beaver Dams. At this time the Americans were in full possession of Niagara and the frontier as far as Queenston with an outpost at St. Davids and strong pickets out at all available points. The British Army at Niagara under General Vincent after their defeat by the Americans under Gen. Dearborn had retreated to Burlington Heights and there established themselves with outposts at Jordon, under Col. Bishop and at a point near Homer under Major DeHaren. A small party consisting of about 50 men of the 49th Regt. under Lieut. Fitzgibbon and about 100 Indians under Capt. Ducharme were also stationed at the Beaver Dams. Such was the situation of affairs where our story commences. That story is the record of a brave woman whose deed of daring and through whose information the British Commander was enabled to achieve a signal victory and to be the means under Divine Providence of saving Upper Canada to the British Crown. Lieut. Fitzgibbon and his detachment had been most active in annoying the enemy, and to get rid of him and at the same time obtain an advantageous base of operations against Gen. Vincent's position on Burlington Heights, it was resolved by the American Commander to capture the Lieut. and the British position at the Beaver Dams. This course was adopted at a Council of War held at Fort George on the 18th of June, 1813. To carry out this determination the American General selected a force of about 650 men composed of about 400 light Infantry, two companies of mounted Infantry, a company of Artillery with two field pieces, and a half troop of Cavalry and placed them under the command of Col. Boerstler, an officer noted for his bravery and distinguished for gallantry during the Indian wars.

Heroine Laura Secord.

As I before stated, the village of Queenston was in possession of the Americans and but few of the older inhabitants remained there. Among the few was the heroine of this story, Laura Secord, and her husband. Mr. Secord was still suffering and helpless from the wound he received at the Battle of Queenston. At their house the American officers were billeted and among them was Col. Boerstler. On June 23rd while these officers were at dinner the Colonel talked freely of his intended enterprise—told of his plans to capture Fitzgibbon and his small party at the Beaver Dams. How a base of operations would then be had for the advance on the position held by the British at Burlington. "That position once captured—shouted the gallant Colonel, and Upper Canada is ours." Laura Secord listened to all this, and when the officers retired from the house to perform their several duties and Col. Boerstler had gone in the direction of Niagara to join his command for the capture of Fitzgibbon, she consulted with her husband as to the best course to pursue—some one must go to warn Fitzgibbon, she said—Mr. Secord could not go, and there was no other to send and she resolved to go herself. She did not for a moment hesitate. Her courage rose to meet the emergency. Bidding her husband and children a hurried farewell, she, in the early evening of the 23rd, left her home for a long and perilous walk to the Beaver Dams.

With a sunbonnet on her head and a milk pail in her hand she passed the first sentinel and was not challenged. She sped onward and when about two miles from her home she was challenged by another sentinel who roughly demanded to know where she was going. Her story was that she was going to visit a sick brother and with real tears besought the guard not to detain her—after some questioning she was allowed to go on her way. Through the woods she sped along, meeting many adventures by the way until at last she reached the position where was encamped a group of Indians who at once made her a prisoner. She asked to be taken to their chief. They complied with her request and she at once made herself known and demanded to be led to Lieut. Fitzgibbon for whom she said she had great news. After some hesitation she was taken to Fitzgibbon's quarters and at once told her story. He realized its importance. "Mrs. Secord." he said, "you have save me and you have saved Vincent, God bless you." After seeing Mrs. Secord comfortably housed for the night the Lieutenant took his measures to give the enemy a warm reception. Posting his little army in advantageous position and out of sight of an advancing enemy and directing Gen. Ducharme to post his Indians, in a ravine in the Beech woods which was selected as a good place for an ambuscade, the little band waited for the enemy to appear. About 9 o'clock the Americans appeared and were received by a steady and incessant fire from the woods on every side. Boerstler ordered the artillery to open fire on the woods, but this was ineffectual and the repeated attempts to march forward were repulsed, Boerstler several times changed direction, meeting each time an invisible enemy. Believing himself to be surrounded by a large force of the British and seeing no other alternative he at last sent up a flag of truce with an offer of surrender, which offer was accepted, and articles of capitulation signed. By this surrender Col. Boerstler, twenty-three officers and five hundred and seventy-five men became prisoners of war. Besides were surrendered the colors of the 14th U. S. Infantry, two cannons, two baggage wagons and about 600 stand of arms as substantial tokens of victory. Laura Secord remained at DeCew's house until the 25th when Lieut. Fitzgibbon had her conveyed home. Her return was a happy one as her purpose had been achieved and the results beyond the most sanguine expectations. I cannot close this brief narrative without recalling an incident of the Battle of Queenston. Mrs. Secord and family were living there at that time and Mr. Secord was one of the party that conveyed the remains of the dead Brock from the place where he fell to the stone house where he lay until taken to Fort George in the afternoon. Mr. Secord returned to take his share of the battle and while following gallant McDonnell up the heights received a severe wound on the shoulder. Intelligence of this occurrence reached Mrs. Secord and she at once hurried to his side. Just as she arrived three American soldiers arrived and raising their muskets were about to club him to death. Rushing between them she threw herself on the body of her husband, thus shielding him and implored the ruffians to spare her husband's life. With rough words they pushed her aside and were about to accomplish their murderous intent, when Capt. Wool of the American army came up, and calling them cowards sternly demanded how they dared do such a thing. He had them arrested and sent to Lewiston where they were afterwards court-martialed and as a result received well merited imprisonment for several months for their infamous breach of discipline. Captain Wool ordered a party of men to take Mr. Secord to his home, and did not even make him a prisoner on parole. Captain Wool never forgot the friend he made that day. He rose to the high rank of Major General and visited Mr. Secord several times, and their friendship continued until Mr. Secord's death. This same Captain Wool stationed a guard at the stone house where the dead body of Brock was conveyed, to protect it from injury and insult. It is pleasant amid the horrors and cruelties of war to record the noble actions of a generous foe. Mr. Secord and family lived at Queenston for many years, when recieving a government appointment, he removed to Chippawa where he died in 1842. Laura Secord still continued to reside at Chippawa and died in 1868 in the 95th year of her age. In 1860 she was presented to H. R. H., the Prince of Wales, and her brave exploit brought to his notice. He afterwards generously sent her his check for £100, but no acknowledgement of her services was made by the government. She left six children, five daughters and one son, none of whom are now living. Her only son purchased the stone house hallowed by the presence of the dead warrior and lived there until he removto Niagara. Laura Secord and her husband are buried in the old cemetery on Drummond Hill. A simple stone marks the spot where this true hearted couple sleeps. This burying ground was the battle field of Lundy's Lane and many of the dead that fell in that fierce conflict mingle their dust with theirs.

A General Campaign.

During this time, and for more than three months, the main body remained for the most part inactive, and entrenched at Fort George, under the command successively of Generals Dearborn, Lewis, Boyd and Wilkinson. The duty of foraging devolved upon Colonel Scott, which he did at least twice a week. In these excursions repeated skirmishes with small parties of the enemy occurred. Not a load of forage was cut between the hostile camps without a sharp combat, in which Scott always came off victorious.

In September an expedition was planned against Burlington Heights, at the head of Lake Ontario, reported to be the depot of a large quantity of provisions and other British stores. In this expedition Col. Scott volunteered to command the land troops, and was taken on board the fleet by Commodore Chauncey. Burlington Heights were visited, but neither enemy nor stores were found there. On the return it was determined to make a descent upon York (now Toronto). Accordingly a landing of the soldiers and marines was affected, under the command of Col. Scott. The barracks and public storehouses were burnt. Large depots of provisions and clothing were taken, together with eleven armed boats, and a considerable quantity of ammunition and several pieces of cannon.

At the close of this summer a plan of campaign was devised, having for its object Kingston, and then Montreal. Without going into the details of the objects of this plan and the movements of the different armies, we will simply say, that in accordance with the plan, Wilkinson embarked with the Niagara army on the 2nd day of October, leaving Colonel Scott commander of Fort George with between seven and eight hundred regulars, with a part of Col. Swift's regiment of militia, to defend the Fort. And as this fort had been taken by Col. Scott and the British colors taken down by his own hands, he was proud of the capture, and determined to defend it as the post of honor. He lost not a moment nor an effort to improve the defences of the fort. Expecting an assault at any moment, all hands, including the commander, worked night and day. A week accomplished much, at the end of which, (Oct. 9th), the enemy, contrary to all expectations, broke up his camp, burning three thousand blankets, many hundred stand of arms, also the blankets in the men's packs, and ever article of clothing not in actual use and then followed Wilkinson down the country. On the 13th of October, 1813, by order of Major-General Wilkinson, Col. Scott left Fort George, with the whole of the regular troops of the garrison, being relieved by Brigadier-General McClure, with a body of the New York detached militia, expecting to embark at the mouth of Genesee River, where Wilkinson was to provide means for his embarkation, but failed to do so, so that he had to march to Sackett's Harbor, through rain and mud.

On the 12th of November the expedition down the St. Lawrence for the conquest of Canada was abandoned, and the army commenced a retreat. Sir George Provost being relieved from his apprehension of an attack on Montreal, ordered his forces under Generals Vincent and Drummond, to proceed to Niagara. The Americans had left this frontier defenseless, except about 60 men of the New York Militia who were left to garrison Fort George. Being hard pressed by the enemy, McClure concluded to abandon the post. So on the 10th of December he left for Fort Niagara, after, through a misconception of his orders, he burned the village of Newark, and the people, who were noncombatants, were turned out into a deep snow, in intensely cold weather. The British officers resolved to retaliate, although the act was promptly disavowed by the American Government.

British Cross the Border.

On the night of December 18th 1,000 British and Indians crossed the river at "Five Mile Meadow," shooting and plundering the inhabitants and laying low the whole Frontier to Buffalo. Col. Murray, with 550 regulars, turned toward the Fort of Niagara, prepared to storm it. The pickets were captured without giving any alarm, and the enemy on reaching the fort about three o'clock in the morning actually found the main gate standing open and undefended, and the fortress at their mercy. For a few minutes the "south-eastern blockhouse" and the "red barracks" withstood the entrance of the foe so stoutly that several were killed or wounded, among the latter was Col. Murray. Most of the 450 occupants of the Fort only awoke to find themselves prisoners The slight resistance was made the pretext for an inhuman onslaught in which 80 of the helpless garrison, including many hospital patients, were slaughtered after surrendering. Fourteen were wounded, 344 taken prisoner, 20 escaped; 27 cannon, 3000 stand of small arms, and great quantities of ammunition, provisions and camp equipage fell into the hands of the victors. They held the fort until the treaty of peace restored it.

The portion of the British forces which did not accompany Col. Murray to the fort, including the Indians, pillaged and destroyed the six or eight houses then constituting Youngstown. They then marched upon Lewiston, where they plundered, burned and butchered to their hearts content. Mr.

Lossing understood that 500 Indians under General Riall crossed from Queenston to Lewiston on hearing a cannon fired at Fort Niagara announcing its capture. He quotes the following extract of a letter from an officer of high rank, (whom he conjectures to have been General Drummond) at Queenston, written while the devastation was going on:

"A war-hoop from five hundred of the most savage Indians (which they gave just at daylight, on hearing of the success of the attack on Fort Niagara) made the enemy (at Lewiston) take to their heels, and our troops are in pursuit. We shall not stop until we have cleared the whole frontier. The Indians are retaliating the conflagration of Newark. Not a house within my sight but is in flames. This is a melancholy but just retaliation."

Mr. Lossing, who quotes this letter, remarks: "Fearful was the retaliation for the destruction of half-inhabited Newark, where not a life was sacrificed! Six villages, many isolated country houses and four vessels were consumed, and the butchery of innocent persons at Fort Niagara, Lewiston, Schlosser, Tuscarora Village, Black Rock and Buffalo, and in farm houses, attested the fierceness of the enemy's revenge."

But it is impossible to give the reader such an account of the condition of things on the Niagara frontier, during that ill-fated winter as will enable him to realize the alarm, the panic, and the calamities that prevailed on every hand, and of the sufferings that were endured by the pioneers on the border.

Perry on Lake Erie.

On September 10th of this year, 1813, an exciting battle took place on one of those inland seas which separate the possessions of the two governments. The American fleet on Lake Erie, which had been formed during the past summer, was under the command of Commodore Oliver Hazard Perry. It now consisted of the Niagara and Lawrence, each mounting twenty-five guns, and several smaller vessels, carrying on an average of two guns each. The enemy's fleet was considered of equal force. Commodore Barclay, its commander, was a veteran officer, while Perry was young and without experience as a commander. The battle began on the part of the Americans about 12 o'clock at noon. Perry's flag ship, the Lawrence, being disabled, he embarked in an open boat, and amidst a shower of bullets, carried the ensign of command on board of the Niagara, and once more bore down upon the enemy with the remainder of the fleet. The action became general and severe, and at four o'clock the whole British squadron, consisting of six vessels, carrying in all sixty-three guns, surrendered to the Americans. In giving information of his victory to General Harrison, Perry wrote: "We have met the enemy, and they are ours."

This success on lake Erie opened a passage to the territory which had been surrendered by General Hull; and General Harrison lost no time in transferring the war thither. On the 22d of September, he landed his troops near Fort Malden, but to his surprise, instead of an armed force, he met, at the entrance of the town, the maids and matrons of Amherstburg, who, in their best attire, had come forth to solicit the protection of the Americans.

American Citizens Impressed.

In October, 1807 Great Britain, by proclamation, recalled from foreign service all seamen and sea-faring men who were natural born subjects, and ordered them to withdraw themselves and return home. At the same time it declared that no foreign letters of naturalization could divert its natural-born subjects of their allegiance, or alter their duty to their lawful sovereign.

In the United States, by the act of naturalization, a foreigner becomes entitled to all the privileges and immunities of natural born citizens, except that of holding several offices, such as President and Vice-President. The two positions were those of absolute antagonism, and were alone sufficient to account for much of the controversy and heat which attended the war of 1812. Claims to the reclamation of British-born subjects naturalized in America, and claims to impress them when found in American ships, were made on the one hand and resisted on the other. This was the state of things when the incidents took place which we are about to relate.

The battle of Queenston closed with the surrender of Scott and his small force to the greatly superior numbers under the command of General Sheaffe. These prisoners were sent to Quebec, thence in a cartel to Boston. When the prisoners were about to sail from Quebec, Scott, being in the cabin of the transport, heard a bustle upon deck, and hastened up. There he found a party of British officers in the act of mustering prisoners, and separating from the rest such as, by confession or the accent of the voice, were judged to be Irishmen. The object was to send them, in a frigate then alongside, to England, to be tried and executed for the crime of high treason, they being taken in arms against their native allegiance. Twenty-three had been thus set apart when Scott reached the deck, and there were at least forty more of the same birth in the detachment. They were all in deep affliction at what they regarded as the certain prospect of a shameful death. Many were adopted citizens of the States, and several had families in the land of their adoption. The moment Scott ascertained the object of the British officers, acting under the express orders of the Governor-General, Sir. George Provost, he commanded his men to answer no more questions, in order that no other selection should be made by the test of speech. He commanded them to remain absolutely silent, and they strictly obeyed. This was done in spite of the threats of the British officers, and not another man was separated from his companions. Scott was repeatedlyly commanded to go below, and high altercations ensued. He addressed the party selected, and explained to them fully the reciprocal obligations of allegiance and protection, and assuring them that the United States would not fail to avenge their gallant and faithful soldiers; and finally pledged himself, in the most solemn manner, that retaliation, and, if necessary, a refusal to give quarter in battle, should follow the execution of any one of the party. In the midst of this animated harangue he was frequently interrupted by the British officers, but, though unarmed, could not be silenced.

The Irishmen, whose names were as follows: Henry Kelley, Henry Blaney, George McCommon, John Dalton, Michael Condin, John Clark, Peter Burr, Andrew Doyle, John McGowan, James Gill, John Fulsom, Patrick Mc-Braharty, Matthew Mooney, Patrick Karns, John Fitzgerald, John Wiley, John Donelly, John Curry, Nathan Shaley, Edward McGarrigan, John Dinnue, John Williams, George Johnson, were put in irons on board the frigate and sent to England. When Scott landed in Boston, he proceeded to Washington and was duly exchanged. He immediately related to the President the scene which had occurred at Quebec, and was by him instructed to make a full report of the whole transaction, in writing, to the Secretary of War. This was done on the 13th of January, 1813. The result was that on March 3rd, 1813, an act was passed vesting the President of the United States with the power of retaliation.

Two months after this (May 27th, 1813,) in the battle and capture of Fort George, Scott made a great number of prisoners. True to his pledge given at Quebec, he, as Adjutant-General, (chief of staff) immediately selected twenty-three of the number to be confined in the interior of the United States, there to abide the fate of the twenty-three imprisoned and sent to England by the British officers. In making this selection he was careful not to include a single Irishman, in order that Irishmen might not be sacrificed for Irishmen. This step led, on both sides, to the confinement as hostages of many other men and officers, all of whom were, of course, dependent for their lives on the fate of the original twenty-three.

In July 1815, when peace had been months concluded, and Scott (then a a major-general) was passing along on the East River side of the city of New York, he was attracted by loud cheers and bustle on one side of the piers. He approached the scene and great was his delight to find that it was the cheers of his old Irish friends, in whose behalf he had interfered at Quebec, and who had that moment landed in triumph, after a a confinement of more than two years in English prisons. He was quickly recognized by them, hailed as their deliverer, and nearly crushed by their warm-hearted embraces. Twenty-one were present, two having died natural deaths.

The Army Disciplined.

The campaign of 1813 ended in disgrace and disaster. The hopes of the nation which had been excited by the brilliant achievements with which it opened, sank to despair, when the army, after sustaining a partial defeat, made an abrupt and hasty retreat.

Amidst the disasters of the campaign there was one benefit. The touch-stone of experience had been applied to the temper of the army, and it was now easy to take the pure metal from the dross. It was a hard school of adversity; but many a brave and highly gifted young man was trained by its teachings to become an accomplished and efficient officer. On the other hand it detected the emptiness and unfitness of many a fop, both young and old, who had been seduced into the service by the glitter of uniform and the pomp of military parade. They were made to learn and feel their incompetency to endure the duties or the frowns of war. An elegant writer has well remarked, that the rude winter gales of Canada swept from our ranks the painted insects, which were fit only to spread their glittering wings in the summer sun; but, at the same time aroused and invigorated the eagle-spirits, which during the calm cower in solitude and silence, but, as the tempest rises, come forth from obscurity to stem the storm and sport themselves in the gale.

The military spirit of the army was lost. New levies of troops were to be made and the spirit of daring, of confidence and energy, was to be created before they could take the field.

To accomplish these objects, Colonel Scott, who, on the 9th of March, 1814, was promoted to the rank of Brigadier-General, immediately joined Major-General Brown, then marched with the army from the French Mills towards the Niagara Frontier.

The army was rapidly assembled at Buffalo. It consisted at that time of Scott's brigade, Ripley's brigade, Hindman's battalion of artillery (all regulars,) and Gen Porter's brigade of militia.

Scott's brigade consisted of the battalions of the 9th, the 11th and the 25th regiments of infantry, with a detachment of the 22nd, and Tonson's company of artillery. The brigade of Gen. Ripley was composed of the 1st, 21st and 23rd infantry. Porter's command was composed of bodies known as Canadian Volunteers, New York Volunteers and Pennsylvania Volunteers. The signal services rendered at a subsequent period, and the glory which they won for their country on hard-fought battle-fields, renders it proper that we should record and remember names so justly distinguished in history.

These troops were placed in the school of instruction at Buffalo, where for three months they were drilled in all the evolutions and tactics necessary to give them the most accurate and thorough discipline. Officers and men were taught the proper distribution of duties between each other, between the different corps, and the different services, from the formation of a column of attack to the presentation of a salute, and to the exchange of the minutest courtesies. It is said that Scott, while at Buffalo observed a captain passing a sentinel posted. The sentinel saluted him by carrying arms, making his musket ring with the action. The captain passed without acknowledging the salute of the soldier. Gen. Scott sent an aide to him to say, that he (the captain) would take care to repass the sentinel in 20 minutes, and repair the fault, or take a trial before a court martial.

The value of discipline, of obedience, and of personal skill in their business, thus acquired by the troops of an army, cannot be over-estimated For want of it, the brave and gallant, but undisciplined volunteers of patriot armies have been scattered and driven by veteran soldiers fighting in a worse cause, and having far less of moral motive to sustain them. With it soldiers of despots have fought with invincible firmness, choosing graves where they stood, to life in retreat. The armies of Suwarraw would fall in the ranks, but without orders never retreat.

The troops of Great Britain are well disciplined; and it was in the sharpest contest with them that the army of Niagara soon proved how much it had gained in the camp of instruction at Buffalo.

The apparent though not unprofitable inactivity which had pervaded the American army of the north, during the spring of 1814, disappeared before the rising heat of the summer sun. In the latter part of June General Brown returned to Buffalo, and thenceforward the storm of war, with its hurried tramp, its loud clangor, its heroic deeds and its untimely deaths, was heard swiftly sweeping along the shores of the Niagara.

Capture of Fort Erie.

Early in the morning of the 3rd of July, 1814, Scott's brigade, with the artillery corps of Major Hindman, crossed the river and landed below Fort Erie, while Ripley's brigade landed above. Scott led the van, crossing in a boat with Colonel Camp, who had volunteered his services, and was on the shore before the enemy's piquet fired a gun. The British garrison of Fort Erie consisted of parts of the 8th and 100th regiments. It soon surrendered and 170, including seven officers, were taken prisoners, and sent to the American side. Preparations were immediately made to advance and attack the army of General Riall at Chippawa.

The Battle of Chippawa.

On the morning of the Fourth, Scott's brigade moved towards Chippawa, and for 16 miles he had a running fight with the Marquis of Tweedale, who commanded the British 100th regiment, 'till at dusk the latter was driven across Chippawa Creek, and joined the main body of the British army under General Riall. The Marquis has since said that he could not account for the order of the pursuit until he recollected the fact that it was the American great anniversary.

The positions of the British and of the Americans on the 5th of July may be easily understood. On the east side was the Niagara River, and near it the road to Chippawa. On the west was a heavy wood. Between these, running from the woods to the river, were two streams, the principal of which was Chippawa Creek. The other was a small stream above, known in history as Street's Creek. Behind, and below Chippawa Creek, lay the army of General Riall, with a heavy battery on one side and a block house on the other. Scott's brigade had rested for the night on and above Street's Creek. Over these streams the road to Chippawa passed on bridges, the one over Street's near the Americans and the other over the Chippawa near the British. This was the position of the respective parties on the morning of the 5th when General Brown was expecting to attack the British, and they in turn determined to anticipate it, by a sortie from the lines of Chippawa. It was a long day in summer; the earth was dry and dusty, and the sun bright and hot when the best troops of Britain and America met, as in tournaments of old, to test their skill, their firmness, and their courage on the banks of the Niagara.

The day began with the skirmishes of light troops. The British militia and the Indians occupied the wood on the Americans left, and about noon annoyed the American piquets placed on the flank. General Porter, with volunteers, militia and some friendly Indians of the Six Nations, soon engaged them, and, after some skirmishing, drove them through the wood back upon Chippawa. Here the British, finding that their main army under General Riall was advancing, rallied, and in turn attacked

Porter, compelling his command to give way. In spite of his own efforts and personal gallantry, these light troops broke and fled, at sight of the formidable array of Riall.

It was now about four o'clock. General Brown was then in the woods with Porter; when a cloud of dust arose toward Chippawa, and firing was heard. This apprised him that the British army was advancing. At this very moment, Gen. Scott, in ignorance of the British advance, was moving his brigade towards the plain, simply for the purpose of drill. Near the bridge over Street's Creek he met General Brown, who said, "the enemy is advancing. You will have a fight." Gen. Brown passed to the rear, to put Ripley's brigade in motion, and to reassemble the light troops behind Street's Creek. It was not till he arrived at the bridge, over Street's Creek, 200 yards to the right of his camp of the night before, that Scott saw the enemy. The army of Riall had crossed the bridge over Chippawa Creek, and displayed itself on the plain before described. It was composed of the 100th regiment under Lieutenant-Colonel Marquis of Tweedale, the 1st or Royal Scots under Lieutenant-Colonel Gordon, a portion of the 8th or King's regiment, a detachment of the Royal Artillery, a detachment of the Royal 19th Light Dragoons, and a portion of Canada militia and Indians. The main body of these troops were among the best in the British army.

This force was supported by a heavy battery of nine pieces, within point blank range of the American troops. Under the fire of this battery the corps of Scott passed the bridge in perfect order but, with some loss. His first and second battalions, under Majors Leavenworth and McNeil, after crossing formed a line to the front, which brought them opposed respectively to the left and centre of the enemy. The third battalion under Major Jesup obliqued in column to the left, and advanced to attack the right of the enemy, which extended into the woods. Captain Towson with his artillery was stationed on the right, resting in the road to Chippawa.

Without going into further detail we would simply say that the action now became general. Major Jesup now in the woods, and out of view, engaged and held in check the enemy's right wing. The plain widened on the flank, and the enemy's main line continued to advance. Jessup having thus held in check one battalion in the woods, the engagement there gave the enemy a new right flank upon the plain. General Scott, who had continued alternately to advance and fire, was now not more than 80 paces from the enemy. The enemy having a new flank, Scott took advantage of the enlarged interval between Leavenworth and McNeil, to throw the left flank of McNeils's battalion forward on its right, so that it stood obliquely to the enemy's charge and flanked him a little on his new right. At this moment, Gen. Scott called aloud to McNeil's battalion, which had not a recruit in it: "The enemy says that we are good at a long shot, but cannot stand the cold iron. I call upon the Eleventh instantly to give the lie to that slander. Charge!" This movement was executed with decisive effect. A corresponding charge was also made by Leavenworth, who held an oblique position on our right. These charges, sustained by the flank fire of Towson's artillery on the right, quickly put the enemy to rout.

In the mean time, and nearly at the same, Major Jesup, commanding the left flank battalion, finding himself pressed in front and flank, ordered his men to "support arms and advance." This order was promptly obeyed amidst a deadly and destructive fire. Having gained a more secure position, he returned so severe a fire as caused them to retire. Thus was the whole British line fairly routed in a field action on an open plain. They fled to their intrenchments beyond Chippawa Creek, hotly pursued by Scott to the distance of half musket shot of Chippawa Bridge. He took many prisoners, leaving the plain behind strewn with the dead and wounded of both nations.

The contending forces on the British side, according to the British Adjutant-General's report, dated the 13th of July, 1814, in giving a return of the killed and wounded, enumerates the 1st regiment, (Royal Scots) the 8th, (Queen's) the 100th, (Marquis of Twedale's) a detachment of Royal 19th, (dragoons) a detachment of artillery and a portion of Canada Militia. These regiments were not full, but altogether numbered about 2,100 men. Of which 138 were killed, 319 wounded and 46 missing; total loss 503.

The American troops were the 8th, 11th and 25th infantry, with a detachment of the 22nd. Towson's artillery and Porter's Volunteers, making 1900 men, all told, of which 60 were killed, 248 wounded and 19 missing, making a total loss of 327, making a grand total loss of 830 from about 4,000 men.

A British officer who wrote at the time said,"Numerous as were the battles of Napoleon, and brave as were his soldiers, I do not believe that he, the greatest warrior that ever lived, can produce an instance of a contest so well maintained, or, in proportion to numbers engaged, so bloody, as that at Chippawa."

The battle was fought on the 5th day of July, 1814, on Chippawa Plains, and was an exciting and in some degree a poetic scene. It was fought at the close of a long, bright, summer day. On one side rolled the waters of the deep blue Niagara, on the other was seen the verdure of the northern forest. The plain on which the hostile forces met was level and smooth, as if prepared for the meeting of the warriors of ancient knighthood. The best troops of England wheeled into it over Chippawa Bridge and the regiments of America, cool and determined, marched to meet them in combat. The sun shone down, and brilliant arms flashed in its beams. Each movement of the troops was distinct. As the battle deepened, fine bands of music mingled their melody, in sudden bursts, with the roar of artillery and the moans of the wounded.

The battle ended and many were the dead on that dusty plain, whose last groans expired with the last rays of the sun. Darkness came on, and wearied with battle and thirsty from heat, each army retired to its camp, the Americans being victorious. The dead woke not from their bloody beds, the living sank to rest.

Battle of Lundy's Lane.

After the campaign of 1813, Fort Messasaugua was erected near the mouth of Niagara river and added to the defences of Fort George. These forts General Riall, the British commander, reinforced and then retired to Burlington Heights, near the head of Lake Ontario, soon after the battle of Chippawa.

On the 10th of July, 1814, the American camp was removed to Queenston, with the view of capturing these defences before commencing any interior operations. To accomplish this object General Brown sent to Sackett's Harbor for heavy cannon, which were to have been transported by the American vessels to the place of action, but as Commodore Chauncey lay sick at the time, and the enemy had a momentary superiority on the lake, the intentions of the commander in regard to the ports at the mouth of the Niagara were disappointed.

Gen. Brown then determined to attack Burlington Heights; but to induce the enemy to descend, and at the same time draw a small supply of provisions from Schlosser, he masked his intentions by feigning a retreat up the Niagara, recrossed Chippawa Creek and encamped.

Had this movement failed to withdraw the British troops from the Heights, it was intended to use the 25th as a day of rest and on the 26th to send General Scott forward by the road from Queenston, and force Riall to action, no matter how strongly he might be posted. But events determined otherwise, and what was intended to be a day of rest, was one of the most active and bloody days of the campaign.

In the afternoon of the 25th, amidst general relaxation, General Brown received a note from a colonel of militia whose regiment occupied two or three posts on the American side of the Niagara, stating in the most precise terms, that the enemy had thrown a thousand men across from Queenston to Lewiston for some reason not exactly understood. But General Brown conjectured that it was the enemy's intention to capture our magazines, and to intercept supplies coming from Buffalo. In order to recall him from this object, Brown immediately determined to threaten the forts at the mouth of the Niagara.

In less than 20 minutes Scott's command was put in motion for that purpose. His force consisted of four small battalions, under Col. Brady, and Majors Jesup, Leavenworth and McNeil, Captain Towson's artillery, and Captain Harris's detachment of regular and volunteer cavalry; in all amounting to 1,300 men. So hurriedly did they start that there was not time to call in the guards belonging to these corps.

About two miles from the camp and just above the Falls, Scott discovered a few British officers, mounted, who as it turned out, were in advance to reconnoitre, and soon learned that the enemy was in some little force below and only intercepted from view by a small wood.

In this situation, General Scott reflected a moment on what course would be best to pursue. He was instructed to march rapidly on the forts, under positive information (given as we have narrated to General Brown,) that Riall had, three hours before, thrown half his force across the Niagara at Lewiston. Reflecting that the whole had been beaten on the 5th inst., he lost no time in reconnoitreing, but dashed forward to disperse what he thought was the remnant of the British army opposed to him.

After dispatching Assistant Adjutant-General Jones to General Brown with the information that the enemy was in front, he proceeded to pass the wood, and was greatly astonished to find directly in front, drawn up in order of battle, on Lundy's Lane with nine pieces of artillery, a larger force than he had encountered at Chippawa 20 days before. The position he was in was extremely critical. To stand fast was out of the question, being already under a heavy fire of the enemies artillery and musketry. To retreat was equally as hazardous; for there is always in such a case the probability of confusion, and at this time the danger of creating a panic in the reserve, then supposed to be coming up, and which had not been in the previous battle.

Scott saw that no measure but one of boldness would succeed. He therefore determined to maintain the battle against superior numbers and positions until the reserve came up, thus giving General Riall the idea that the whole American army was at hand. This would prevent him from profiting by his numerical strength to attack our flanks and rear. He would thus lose the initial, a matter of no small importance in military enterprise. The scheme succeeded, and for a long time the enemy was kept on the defensive, till the American reserve came up and entered into the action.

It appears from General Drummond's report on July 26th, that he thought his position in Lundy's Lane was attacked by the whole American army. He thanks the army for "repulsing the efforts of a numerous and determined enemy to carry the position of Lundy's Lane." But the truth was that the American combatants stood for more than an hour and maintained a contest against a force seven times their number.

In the meanwhile Scott had sent back to General Brown, Lieutenant Douglass, as well as Major Jones, to report the condition of affairs. The first was to report that the remnant of Riall's army was maneouvering to protect the detachment thrown over the Niagara; the second was to inform the general that so far from being diminished, the British army was actually reinforced, and thus to hasten up the reserve.

On the British side the facts were these: In the night before, the night of the 24th, Lieutenant-General Sir Gordon Drummond had arrived, in the British fleet, at the mouth of the Niagara, with a large reinforcement from Kingston and Prescott. This was wholly unknown to General Brown. Drummond had, in advance, sent instructions to Riall to meet him on the 25th, on the Niagara. Accordingly Riall had marched up the very road it had been arranged Scott was to take on the 26th. He had come by Queenston without putting a man over the Niagara. He had continued his route, as the advance of Drummond's army towards the Falls. On the way he had already been joined by two of the battalions which had come up in the fleet. The others arrived successively, at intervals of half an hour or an hour, after the action had commenced.

The battle began about 40 minutes before sunset and like its predecessor at Chippawa was the closing drama of a long and warm summer's day. And like that, too, it signalized among the affairs of men a spot which in the world of nature had been rendered illustrious by one of the great and glorious works of God.

When the battle was about to begin just as the setting sun sent his red beams from the west, they fell upon the spray, which continually goes up, like incense, from the deep, dashing torrent of Niagara. The bright light was divided into its primal hues, and a rainbow rose from the waters, encircling the head of the advancing column. In a more superstitious age such a sign would have been regarded, like the Roman auguries, as a precursor of victory. Even now this bow of promise furnished the inspiration of hope, with the colors of beauty.

The sun had now gone down, and darkness came on, but no reinforcements had yet appeared. But the gallant band maintained the battle, although an officer reminded the general that the rule for retiring was accomplished since more than one-fourth of his number was killed or wounded, among whom were many of his officers. The brave Col. Brady had been the first to form his regiment, and on that the loss fell the heaviest. Himself twice wounded, he was entreated, by those who observed him pale from the loss of blood, to quit the field. "Not while I can stand," was the reply, worthy of Leonidas.

It was now nine o'clock. The enemy's right had been driven back from its flank assault with great loss. His left was turned and cut off. His center alone remained firm. It was posted on a ridge and supported by nine pieces of artillery.

Another battalion of Drummond's reinforcements had already arrived, and a fourth one was only a few miles behind. Such was the state of the field when the reinforcements appeared. Gen. Ripley, by whom it was commanded, had been ordered to form his brigade, on the skirt of a wood to the right of Gen. Scott. But, finding that this position was not favorable, he took the responsibility of first moving nearer to the British. For this purpose he was about to pass the brigade of Scott, but coming between him and the enemy, he found that he was suffering severely from their cannon. Ripley then conceived the bold thought of storming the formidable battery. "Col. Miller," said he, "can you take yonder battery?" "I will try," was the answer of that heart of oak—a phrase now familiar to all American lips. At the head of the 21st regiment, he calmly took his course, guided by Gen. Scott, who was perfectly acquainted with the ground, till he had the right direction, marched up to the mouth of the blazing cannon, around which the enemy had rallied, bayonetted the men while firing and possessed himself of their guns. Ripley had moved at the same time, at the head of the 23rd regiment, to the attack of the infantry, and drove them down the eminence, which was the key of of their position.

Here Ripley formed his brigade. Gen. Porter, with his volunteers, was on the right and the artillery of Towson in the center. The enemy rallied in their might and advanced to regain their position and artillery. The Americans perceived that the enemy was coming on, but could not distinctly ascertain from what point. The moon had risen, but dark clouds were in the heavens, and the light was fitful. Sounds came indistinctly mingled from every quarter. The roar of the cataract, the shrieks and groans of the dying and wounded, the discharge of artillery, were all heard, as well as the rush of the enemy's attack. In this situation Ripley gave his troops the order to wait til the enemy's bayonets touched their own, and to take aim by the light from the discharge of their muskets. The aim of the Americans was good and numbers of their brave enemy fell. They closed up their ranks and came on with the bayonet. The Americans stood the charge and sturdily pushed back the thrust. For 20 minutes this deadly strife continued when the veterans of the Duke of Wellington retreated in disorder. But they renewed the attack until they were four times repulsed. At length, about midnight, they ceased to contend, and left their position and artillery to the Americans. Although the brunt of the battle was on the eminence, other efforts were being made in different parts of the field. The brigade of Scott, shattered as it was, having formed anew, was not content to look idly on, while their brethern, who had stepped between them and death, were now bleeding in their turn. Gen. Scott charged at their head, through an opening in Ripley's line, but in the confusion and darkness of the scene, he passed between the fires of the combatants. He afterwards in the fight took his post on Ripley's left. In another quarter, Col. Jessup, with only 200 men, advanced upon the enemy, brought them to close action, drove them from the ground and captured Gen. Riall with other officers and soldiers to a number almost equal to his own.

Major Ketchum, of the 25th regiment of infantry, was the officer who personally made Gen. Riall a prisoner. The British general was brought to Scott by Major Ketchum, and directions were given that the distinguished prisoner be taken to the rear, and treated with the greatest possible kindness. Riall, badly wounded, lay some days in the same house in Williamsville, with Scott, yet more severely crippled.

The latter as a special favor, obtained permission from our government, for Riall to return to England on parole, and the same permission for Riall's friend, Major Wilson, also badly wounded, captured at Chippawa. Such favors were, however, at that time only granted by the American government; Sir George Prevost and the British ministry never consented to place on parole or to exchange a prisoner after the Americans confined the 23 hostages in 1813.

In this sanguinary contest the total loss of the British was 878. Generals Drummond and Riall were among the wounded. The American loss in killed, wounded and missing was 860. Of these 11 officers were killed, among whom were Major McFarland and Captain Ritchie. Fifty-six officers were wounded, among whom were Generals Brown and Scott; it was not, however, until towards the close of the action that the two officers highest in command were disabled. Gen. Brown, on receiving his wound, gave notice to Gen. Ripley that he was left in command, but ordered him to collect the wounded, remove the artillery and retire to the camp at Chippawa.

General Brown in his official report said, "While retiring from the field, I saw and felt that the victory was complete on our part, if proper measures were promptly adopted to secure it. The exhaustion of the men was, however, such as made some refreshments necessary. They particularly required water."

Unfortunately the Americans lost the trophies of their hard-earned victory as no means of removing the captured artillery were at hand, and General Ripley was obliged to leave it on the field of battle. The British on learning that the Americans had abandoned the field, re-occupied it immediately, and taking advantage of this circumstance, their officers in their dispatches to their government boastfully claimed the victory.

The world has seen mightier armies moved over more memorable fields and followed by louder reports of the far resounding trumpet of fame; a bloodier scene for those engaged, a severer test of courage and of discipline, or one whose action was more closely associated with the sublime and beautiful in nature the world has not seen. The armies were drawn out near the shores of that rapid river whose current mingles lake with lake, and hard by was that cataract whose world of waters rushes over the precipice, and, rushing, roars into the gulf below. The ceaseless spray rises like incense to the Eternal Father. The beams of sun, moon and stars fall ceasely on that spray and are sent back in many colored hues to the source of light. So it was when wheeling into the field of battle the slant rays of the setting sun returning from the spray encircled the advancing column with rainbow colors. The sun went down, to many an eye, to raise no more on earth.

With the darkness came the greater rage of battle—charge after charge was made. For a time the faint beams of the moon struggled with the smoke and gave a little light to the combatants; but it was but little. The moon itself became obscured, and no light save the rapid flashes of musket and cannon pierced the heavy clouds.

The fight raged in the darkness of the night. From the height on the ridge the battery of the enemy still poured its deadly fire.

It was then that the gallant Miller said: "I will try." It was then that Scott piloted his column through the darkness to Lundy's Lane. It was then that the brave regiment charged to the cannon's mouth. The battery was taken and victory rests with the American army.

It was midnight. The battle is ended. The army faint and weary drags itself from the field. The well sink to their couch to dream of homes far away. The wounded groan in their painful hospital. The dead rest until the last trumpet shall summon them to the last array. The warrior with his garments rolled in blood has left the scene of struggles, pain and death. Some kind friend may have sought him whether dead or alive; but the war-drum has ceased to beat; the artillery ceased to roll; and now the solemn, sonorous fall of Niagara is to the dead their requiem, and to the living their song of glory.

Drummond at Ft. Erie.

Gen. Brown had been taken wounded from the field of Lundy's Lane. Towards the close of the battle, Scott, also twice wounded, was borne out of the action.

General Brown did not, however, at once resign the command. He directed Gen. Ripley to return to camp, after bringing off the dead, the wounded and the artillery. But unfortunately, for the want of horses, harness and drag-ropes, the captured artillery of the enemy was left behind—a circumstance much regretted.

The American army, now reduced to 1,000 men, fell back to Chippawa, and there converted the works thrown up by the enemy into defenses against him. On the report that Gen. Drummond, at the head of 5,000 British, was fast approaching, the American camp was hastily broken up, its position abandoned, and a retreat made to Fort Erie, where they strongly intrenched themselves by making such defences as was in their power. On the 5th of August, by order of Gen. Brown, Brigadier-General Gaines arrived from Sackett's Harbor and took the command.

On the 3rd of August, General Drummond appeared in the neigborhood of Fort Erie, and finding it impossible to carry it by storm, was compelled to commence a regular siege. So between the 3rd and 12th of August, Drummond employed himself in endeavoring to cut off the American's provisions, and in the preparatory measures of opening trenches and establishing batteries. On the morning of the 13th he commenced a cannonade and bombardment. This was continued through the day, renewed on the morning of the 14th and continued until seven o'clock in the evening, but without any serious injury to the American ranks. On that day General Gaines doubled his guards and prepared for an assault. At two o'clock in the morning of the 15th a heavy British column was found approaching Towson's battery, stationed at the northwest angle of the works, where it was received by the cannon of Towson and the musketry under the gallant Major Wood, and was effectually repulsed.

A second attack was also repulsed, when the British column changed its direction and attacked the western angle, with just as little success.

In the mean time the center column under Colonel Drummond, after a sanguinary conflict, succeeded in scaling the walls and taking possession of the exterior bastions of the old fort.

While this savage man was denying mercy to the conquered Americans, a quantity of cartridges in a small stone building within the bastion, exploded scattering death and confusion around and expelling the British from the fort. They suffered severely, having left behind a large number of killed, wounded and prisoners. According to the British official report their loss on this day was 57 killed, of whom were Colonels Scott and Drummond, 313 wounded and 539 missing. The total loss of the Americans was but 84.

In fine, the British were most gallantly and effectually defeated in their attempt to storm Fort Erie.

After this repulse, both armies remained in a state of inactivity for some time. General Gaines having been wounded by the bursting of a shell, the command again devolved on General Ripley.

Sortie From Ft. Erie.

On the 2nd of September, General Brown, though not yet fully recovered from the wounds received at Lundy's Lane, resumed the command of his division. After a full examination of the topographical position of Drummond's lines, he thought that a bold and vigorous sortie would be more than mere defence in relieving the American army from the siege of the enemy. Accordingly, on the morning of the 17th of September General Brown, paraded his troops, to the number of about 2,000, in nearly equal proportion of regulars and militia, for a sortie on the enemy's works. The army of Sir Gordon Drummond had then infested Fort Erie for 45 days. During that time they had erected regular lines and batteries. They had bombarded the American defences and made an unsuccessful attack upon them. At this time they had erected two batteries and were about two open a third. Their forces were divided into three brigads, each of which in turn guarded the batteries, while the other two were encamped about two miles distant, out of reach of the American cannon, but near enough to support the troops at the batteries.

In this position of affairs General Brown determined to storm the batteries, destroy the cannon and defeat the brigade. So at 2.30 p. m. of the 17th of August General Porter left the camp at the head of a detachment to penetrate a passage through the woods. Being perfectly acquainted with the ground, he with his men, trod silently and circuitously along, when, arriving at their destined point, they rushed upon the enemy and so successful was the enterprise that in 30 minutes batteries No. 2 and 3 were in the possession of the Americans with two block houses. Soon after battery No. 1 was abandoned and the magazine of No. 3 blown up. The cannon were spiked or dismantled and the garrison taken prisoners, but the brave Colonels Gibson and Wood had fallen at the head of their columns.

So great was the British loss that it became apparent that the siege of Fort Erie could not be protracted with any hope of success.

Accordingly, Lieut.-General Drummond broke up his camp during the night of the 21st of September and returned to his intrenchments behind Chippawa Creek.

Soon after this, the arrival of General Izard placed the Americans on a footing which once more enabled them to commence offensive operations; and leaving Fort Erie in command of Colonel Hindman, General Brown again advanced towards Chippawa. Near this place an affair occured on the 20th of October in which Colonel Bissell, with a detachment of 1,000 men, gained an advantage over a detachment of 1,200, under the Marquis of Tweedale.

On the 10th of November the American army abandoned and destroyed Fort Erie, crossed the river and retired into winter quarters at Buffalo, when the war on the Niagara Frontier was in fact ended.

Resume.

During the year 1814 there had been a succession of brilliant military actions, and much courage, skill and energy exhibited. Taken all in all, no campaign in American history has displayed more of the qualities of mind and body, art and science, which are more to the character of a true soldier or the success of an army in action. In a little less than three months the army of Riall and Drummond, twice renewed and reinforced by troops from Europe, had been defeated in four pitched battles.

In the descriptions we have given of the several, the numbers engaged on either side are stated in each one, as near as the materials preserved by history will allow us to estimate.

The following table will show the total loss in killed, wounded and prisoners taken by each army in the different battles:

	American Loss.	British Loss.
Battle of Chippawa, fought July 5th, 1814	328	507
Battle of Lundy's Lane, fought July 25th, 1814.	860	878
Assault on Fort Erie, August 15th, 1814	84	815
Sortie from Fort Erie, September 17th, 1814	511	900
	1783	3100

If the total number of troops engaged in the several battles on both sides was about 12,000, it follows that nearly one half were among the killed, wounded and prisoners, which is a loss exceeding, in proportion, that of the most bloody battles of Napoleon.

Burning of the Caroline.

Although England had governed the Canadas with great moderation, yet in 1837 by the instigation of W. L. McKenzie, a party arose, who claiming independence, passed from secession to armed revolt. And when the flame of insurrection was kindled in Canada, it was not arrested by a mere line of jurisdiction; but it reached and agitated the frontier inhabitants of the United States, along the border from the hills of Vermont to the Huron of the northwest. On the frontier, the citizens enrolled themselves as Canadian patriots or sympathizers until many of the inhabitants capable of bearing arms were professed friends and abettors of the Canadian movement. Thousands met in lodges along the border, oaths of secrecy were administered, principles appointed, general and staff officers chosen, and, at least for Upper Canada, a provisional government formed. The President of the United States issued his proclamation enjoining all good citizens to observe the strictest neutrality towards the British provinces, but it had little effect.

The arms in the hands of the citizens and even those in the State arsenals within reach of the borders, were soon seized or purloined, thus affording equipments to the Canadian patriots. A Mr. Van Reussellear, with some 700 followers crossed from Schlosser, two miles above Niagara Falls, and took possession of Navy Island on the British side of Niagara River.

This idle invasion, though unimportant to the Canadas, was not without its consequences in history. It was followed by a very serious incident, which excited deep feeling in the United States, and was the subject of much diplomatic correspondence.

A small steamer called the Caroline, which was built at Charleston, S. C., in 1822, and had a capacity of 45 tons, was brought to New York, thence by river and canal to Lake Ontario, where she was employed for some time as a ferry boat. She was then taken through the Welland Canal to Lake Erie, and employed upon the Detroit River. In the summer of 1837 she was seized for smuggling, taken to Buffalo and sold. It was then that she was engaged by Van Rensselear to act as a ferry-boat between Schlosser and Navy Island. But the very night the Caroline commenced her voyages between these two points, one hundred and fifty armed men from the Canada side, in five boats with muffled oars, proceeded to Schlosser, cut the Caroline loose from her moorings, and setting her on fire let her drift over the falls. She happened to be full of idle people, including boys, not connected with Van Rensselear, but who had been attracted to the frontier by the rumor of war, and who had simply begged a night's lodging. One man named Durfee was killed and several others wounded. When this occurred a flame of excitement went up throughout the interior of the United States. The sentiment of patriotism and the feeling of revenge were frequently mingled together, and the peace of this country, and perhaps of all other civilized nations, was threatened by this act of outrage committed on the Caroline.

At that time the question was asked: "Why did the English pass Navy Island in Canada where the patriots had hoisted their flags and waited for them, and attack an unarmed boat in New York State?" At the anniversary dinner in Toronto, in honor of the "heroes" who defeated the Yankees, the Hon. John Emsley, a member of the Head Government was present and said: "After a desperate engagement of some minutes she was fired and rode the waves a blazing beacon of infamy, until she sank into the abyss below. (Loud cheers.) Gentlemen I glory in having been one of those that destroyed this boat." The Montreal Herald of December 29, 1838, said: "Col. Holmers and the officers of his brigade held their first regimental mess dinner at Orr's Hotel. The room was decorated with transparencies of Her Majesty, the Duke of Wellington, Brittania, the steamer Caroline in flames going over the Falls of Niagara, and a globe with the motto: 'The British Empire, on which the sun never sets.' Sir Allan McNab was toasted and many a joke was cracked at the expense of the unfortunate Americans on board the Caroline."

The Caroline was destroyed December 29th, 1837, and the news reached Washington January 4th. A Cabinet meeting was called and General Scott was told that blood had been spilled and he must hasten to the frontier. Full power was give him to call for militia, to put himself in communication with the United States district attorneys, marshalls and collectors in order, through them, to enforce the act of neutrality, the good faith pledged to Great Britain by treaty, and to defend our own territory, if necessary against invasion, or to maintain peace throughout the borders.

In 1812 Scott appeared upon the same theatre as the leader of battalions and the victor of battles. But now, rhetoric and diplomacy were to be his principal weapons, his countrymen and friends his object of conquest, and a little correspondence with the British authorities beyond the line, as an episode to the whole.

In order to shorten this narrative we will not stop to give a history of the wild rumors that were afloat at that time, agitating the minds of the people and keeping them in a constant state of excitement, causing them to get up in the dead hours of the night to flee from some imaginary foe.

Not many days after the burning of the Caroline, another steamer, the Barcelona, was cut out the ice in Buffalo harbor, and taken down the Niagara river to be offered to the patriots, who were still on Navy Island. Scott wished to compel them to discontinue their criminal enterprise. He also desired to have them, on returning within our jurisdiction, arrested by the marshall, who was always with him. For this purpose, he sent an agent to hire the Barcelona for the service of the United States, before the patriots could get means to pay for her, or find sureties to idemify her owners in case of her capture or destruction by the British. He succeeded in all these objects. The Barcelona was taken back to Buffalo, and as she slowly ascended against the current on the American side of Grand Island, three armed British schooners, besides batteries on land were in position, as the day before, to sink her as she came out from behind the island. On the 16th of January, Scott and Gov. Marcy stood on the American shore opposite that point, watching events. The smoke of the approaching boat could be seen in the distance, and the purpose of the British was perfectly evident in all their movements. The batteries on our side were promptly put into position. The matches were lighted. All was ready to return the fire of the British. There was a crisis.

The day before this, when it was supposed the Navy Island people were coming up the same channel in other craft, and before it was known that the Barcelona had accepted his offered engagement, Scott wrote on his knee, and dispatched by an aide-de-camp the following note:

HEADQUARTERS EASTERN DIVISION
U. S. ARMY.
(two miles below Black Rock)
January 15th, 1838.

To the Commander of the Armed British Vessels in the Niagara:

SIR—
With his Excellency the Governor of New York, who has troops at hand, we are here to enforce neutrality of the United States, and to protect our soil and waters from violation. The proper civil authorities are also present to arrest, if practicable, the leaders of the expedition on foot against Upper Canada.

Under these circumstances it gives me pain to perceive the armed vessels mentioned anchored in our waters, with probable intention to fire upon that expedition moving in the same waters.

Unless the expedition should first attack—in which case we shall interfere—we shall be obliged to consider a discharge of shot or shell from or into our waters, from the armed schooners of her Majesty, as an act seriously compromising the neutrality of the two nations. I hope, therefore, that no such unpleasant incident may occur.

I have the honor to remain &c.,
WINDFIELD SCOTT.

The same intimation was repeated and explained the next morning, January 16th, to a captain of the British army, who had occasion to wait upon Scott on other business, and who immediately returned. It was just then that the Barcelona moved up the current of the Niagara. The cannon on either side were pointed, the matches lighted and thousands stood in suspense. On Scott's note and his personal assurance, alone depended the question of peace or war. Happily these assurances had their just effect. The Barcelona passed along. The British did not fire. The matches were extinguished; the two nations, guided by wise counsel resumed their usual way, and war's wild alarms were hushed into the whispers of peace.

The patriots evacuated Navy Island on the 15th inst., and as soon as they landed, Van Rensselaer and his associates were arrested, as Scott said they should be, in his note written a few hours previous to the arrests. A Mr. McLeod was also arrested and tried by a United States court, for the murder of Durfee, but was acquitted.

As small a place as this incident may occupy in history, it was a critical moment in the affairs of nations. Had one British gun been fired, and much more had the Barcelona been destroyed no authority nor influence would have restrained our excited population from taking up arms, and an unpremeditated war would have been the result. It would have been a war from an incident, and not from a national controversy.

In April, 1838, at the annual dinner of the St. George's Society in Canada the flag of the Caroline hung as a trophy behind the president's chair, and the officers present were applauding. Capt. Marryast, the novelist, rose and proposed as a voluntary toast, "Captain Drew and his brave companions who cut out the Caroline." It was received with great applause. On May 20, 1838, the steamboat Sir Robert Peel was burnt at French creek as some retaliation of the Caroline massacre. No lives were taken or even threatened. This was just seven days after Mr. Stevenson, American minister in London, had demanded satisfaction for the Caroline. To show how the act which Americans looked upon as nothing but a base butchery, was received on the other side, it may be said that Capt. Drew was raised to the rank of captain of the royal navy and commanded on Lake Erie. McNab was knighted and received royal thanks, and Sir John Colborne was created Lord Seaton.

The Lewiston Telegraph of Friday, April 19, 1839, printed the following: "John Mosier, late a captain on Lake Ontario, and one of the murderers of Durfee, has presented a petition to the Upper Canadian Parliament praying that land be granted the boarders of the Caroline for a renumeration." Canada, perhaps, is the only country where murderers are recompensed.

The Hermit of Niagara.

In the afternoon of the 18th of June, 1823, a tall, well built and handsome young man, dressed in a long loose gown or cloak of a chocolate color, was seen passing through the principal street of the village of Niagara Falls. He had under his arm a roll of blankets, a flute, a port folio, and a large book; in his right hand he carried a small stick. He advanced towards the Eagle hotel, (which is now part of the International) attracting the gaze of visitors and others by the singularity of his appearance. With elastic step and animated motion, he passed the hotel; he heeded not the inquiring gaze of the idle multitude, but firm and erect he bent his course to a more lowly, but respectable, inn. He at once entered into stipulations with the landlord that the room which he occupied should be solely his own, that he should have his table to himself, and that only certain portions of his fare should be provided by the landlady. He made the usual enquiries about the falls, and, among other things, wished to know if there was a reading room or library in the village. Being informed that there was a library, he immediately repaired to the individual who kept it; deposited three dollars and took a book; purchased a violin; borrowed music books; informed the librarian that his name was Francis Abbott; that he should remain a few days at the Falls, and conversed on many subjects with great ease and ability.

The next day he returned to the same person and; expatiated largely upon the surrounding scenery, the cascades and cataracts, and all of that sublime spectacle, the falls. In all his travels, he said, he had never met with anything to compare with this combination of all that was great and beautiful. There was nothing so grand as Niagara Falls, except Mount Ætna, during an eruption.

He inquired how long travellers usually remained, and being informed that many stayed only one day, he observed that he would stay at least a week, and further remarked; "Can it be that there are those who come to this place and leave it in one day! I am astonished that persons can be found so little interested in these astonishing works of nature, as to spend so short a time in passing around and beholding them. As well might a traveller, in one or two days, attempt to examine in detail the various museums and curiosities in Paris, as to think of becoming acquainted with the magificent scenery of Niagara in such a short space of time."

In a few days he called again, and again expatiated upon the resplendent scenery of the Falls, and said he had concluded to remain a month, and perhaps six months. A short time after, he determined to fix his abode on Goat Island, and was desirous of erecting a rustic hut, for the purpose of abstracting himself from all society and of becoming a solitary hermit. The proprietor of the island, having become acquainted with his eccentricities, was apprehensive that his permanent residence there might be alarming to strangers who did not know him. For this reason he thought it not proper to allow him to erect a buiding for such a purpose, but permitted him to occupy a room in the only house on the island. In this house there lived a family that furnished him at times with milk and bread. But he often dispensed with these necessary articles, providing himself in such other ways as suited himself, and preparing his food to suit his own taste. He observed once to a friend "that people in their mode of living took a great deal of trouble and unnecessary pains; for my part I have adopted a method which I find very pleasant and agreeable. I take about a pint of water in which I mix a sufficient quantity of wheat flour, to give it a proper consistency, and then drink it down. I find that it answers every purpose and saves me much labor and inconvenience.

With his guitar by his side, supported from his shoulder with a silken sash like an eastern minstrel, he would perambulate the banks of the river to the Whirlpool and once or twice he extended his walk to Lewiston.

The inmates of the houses on the way would suddenly hear the sounds of strange and unknown music; the musician would be observed standing at a distance in the road, but as soon as noticed or spoken to he would glide away without giving any reply.

The island was his permanent residence for about one year and eight months. At length the family removed and to those few with whom he held converse, he expressed his great satisfaction to have it in his power to live entirely alone. For some months he seemed to enjoy himself very much, and until another family entered the house.

He then concluded to erect a cottage of his own and as he could not build on the island he chose the high bank near to and in full view of the fall, which of all other objects, it was his delight to behold. He occupied his new residence for about two months.

On Friday, the 10th of June, 1831, he went twice below the bank of the river to bathe and was seen to go a third time. At two o'clock in the afternoon the ferryman saw him in the water—he partly floating and partly resting his body on the shelving rocks. As the boat approached, to screen himself from the gaze of the passengers, he would draw his head under the water. It was not seriously thought of as he had often been noticed in the same situation, and acting in the same manner. When the ferry-man returned, Abbott's clothes were seen on the rocks, where he usually deposited them. An examination was immediately made but his body could not be found. It was supposed to have been carried away by the current.

"The greedy surge had swept him down,
Far, far from mortal ken."

On the 21st of June the body was taken up at Fort Niagara, was clearly identified, and was on the next day removed and decently interred in the burial ground at Niagara Falls from which place it has since been removed to Oakwood Cemetery and a fine tombstone erected to his memory. He and Captain Webb now sleep side by side.

Thus terminated the career of Francis Abbott. Little, indeed, known to those near whom he spent the last two years of his life. A few gleanings can only be given. He was an English gentleman of a respectable family. He was endowed with a good mind, highly cultivated and was pleasing in his manners. He was not only master of several languages, but deeply read in the arts and sciences, and possessed of all the minor accomplishments of the finished gentleman, fascinating colloquial powers, and music and drawing in great perfection.

Many years of his life had been spent in travelling. He had visited Egypt and Palestine; had travelled through Turkey and Greece, Italy, Spain, Portugal and France, and had resided for considerable periods of time in Naples, Rome and Paris. While at Niagara Falls business brought him in contact with several inhabitants. With a few of them he would sometimes be sociable; to all others he was distant and reserved. His conversations were always interesting and his descriptions of countries and people glowing and animated. But at times, even with his favored acquaintances, he would hold no conversation; but communicated to them his wishes on a slate and would request that nothing should be said to him. He would frequently go unshaved for two or three months, often with no covering on his head and his body enveloped in a blanket; shunning all and seeking the deepest solitude of the island. He composed much and generally in Latin; but he destroyed his composition almost as fast as he produced them. When his little cot was examined hopes were entertained that some manuscript or memorial, of his own composition, might be found, but he left nothing of the kind. His faithful dog guarded his door, and it was with difficulty that he was persuaded aside while it was opened. His cat occupied his bed and his guitar, violin, flutes and music were scattered about in confusion. There was a portfolio and the leaves of a large book, but not a word, not even his name was written in any of them.

Many spots of Goat Island are consecrated to the memory of Francis Abbott. On the upper end of the island he had established his walk and it had become trodden and well beaten like that on which a sentinel performs his tour of duty. Between Goat and Moss Islands there was embowered, in seclusion and shade, one of the most charming waterfalls or cascades imaginable. This was his favorite retreat for bathing. There he resorted at all times of the year. In the coldest of weather, even when snow was on the ground, and ice in the water; he continued to bathe in the Niagara.

On the lower extremity of the island there is a bridge leading over what are called the Terrapin Rocks and from this bridge there extended a single piece of timber, some twelve or fifteen feet over the precipice. On this it was his daily practice to walk; with a quick step he would pass the bridge, advance on the timber to the extreme end, turn quickly on his heel and walk back, and continue thus to walk for hours. Sometimes he would let himself down at the end of the timber and hang under it by his hands and feet for 15 or 20 minutes at a time and this over a chasm so terrific as to make dizzy the strongest head. On being remonstrated with for thus exposing himself, he would reply that in crossing the ocean he had frequently seen the sea-boy in much greater peril, and as he should probably cross the ocean again he wished to inure himself to such dangers; if the nerves of others were disturbed, his were not. In the darkest hours of the night he would be found walking alone in the wildest and most dangerous spots near the Falls. At such times he would shun the approach of men as if they were unwelcome intruders on his solitude.

He had a stipend, allowed to him by his friends in England, competent for his support. He attended to the state of his accounts very carefully; was economical in the expenditure of money for his own use; but generous in paying for all favors and services, and never receiving anything without making immediate payment therefore. He had a deep and abiding sense of religious duties and decorum; mild in his behavior and inoffensive in his conduct. Religion was a subject he appreciated, and seemed well to understand. The charity he asked from others he extended to all mankind.

What could have broken up and destroyed such a mind as his? What would drive him from society, which he was so well fitted to adorn—and what should transform him, noble in person and intellect into an isolated anchorite, shunning the associations of his fellow-men. The mystery he never unfolded, and his friends have remained silent on the subject. He was about 28 years of age at the time of his death.

With the scenery of the Falls he was perfectly infatuated and expressed himself in the most rapturous terms, when he spoke of the beautiful retreats of Goat Island. He was asked why he did not take up his residence in Canada, under his own government, among his own people, and, as he preferred being near the falls, he could there select a place to suit him, as the views on that side were considered by many as being the best. He replied that he preferred this side, because, in all that was interesting and beautiful, the American scenes around the falls were decidedly superior.

Avery on the Log.

On the evening of July 18, 1853, a man by the name of Hanniman and one by the name of Avery, in the employ of David Brown, who was engaged in boating sand, left the French landing, (now called Port Day,) for Schlosser where the boat, upon which they were employed, was lying. But for some reason they failed to reach their point, and were carried out into the strong current and down into the rapids. Hanniman was immediately carried over the Falls, but Avery lodged on a log, nearly midway between Goat Island bridge and the fearful precipice. it being the only place in that portion of the rapids upon which a human being could find footing. The fearful truth of a man being in the rapids just above the verge of the Falls was first discovered at about four o'clock on the morning of July 19th by one of the watchmen of the Cataract House. The fearful intelligence spread like a fire alarm throughout the village. Ropes were the first thing thought of—no rope on hand. Messrs. Gage & Haws, contractors on the hydraulic canal, stripped the rigging from their blocks and gin poles. Citizens owning or having in their possession a pound of rope brought it forward.

Boats owned by rich and poor were soon being borne on the shoulders of the multitude to the spot, as an offering of humanity, without a thought of reimbursement. Thus four boats and all the rope in the village were made a freewill offering by the owners to attempt the deliverance of an unknown stranger, but a human being, from a situation as perilous as the human mind can conceive. A telegraph dispatch to Buffalo promptly brought a boat to the spot, the owner not giving the probabilities of remuneration a thought.

Thousands of persons crowded around the scene, each having a plan to which no one heeds but himself. Nothing, absolutely nothing, could be done in this chaotic state. A meeting is proposed on Goat Island bridge by two of the proprietors, to give direction to the efforts about to be made. A vote is taken, and a man is appointed by acclamation, who selects his assistants.

A generous hearted captain from the upper lakes, having heard of the accident at Buffalo hastened down to the scene of action. He was invited to participate in giving direction to the efforts about to be made—he was prompt and efficient. The boat experiment fails—another plan is proposed which is thought feasable—this failed also except to give a knowledge of the currents and the action of water through the different channels—another plan is proposed—ropes were with the life boat—three hundred men man the line attached to the life boat sunken in the rapids—the line parts near the sunken boat and was fortunately brought to shore—the raft is completed and let down into the boiling element from the center of the bridge—(a noble hearted sea captain, a stranger, with a soul stamped with generosity, took one of the managers by the shoulders, and in a whisper, begged for God's sake to let him go down on the raft and help the man keep the ropes clear, and on being refused he replied: "I know I could help him." Generous hearted man! would that the world knew thy name—the original design of the raft is thwarted by one rope being too short to reach the spot, it slips the grasp of those holding it—the raft swings on a line with the remaining rope and bounds down and below the fatal cliff that seemed to stand between life and death—no more rope at hand—nothing daunted the capstan moves on, the raft swings to the embrace of the unfortunate—he reaches the raft and entwines himself among its ropes. He gazes at the pail of provisions lashed to the raft—he cannot eat, he sees nothing but death before him. The raft moves slowly sidewise, under the reef to an almost inaccessible island. The rope becomes entangled among the rocks. What now shall be done? Lower away the raft, now haul her up, now lower her down, the capstan moves the ponderous weight up and down at bidding, a little lower the raft descends into the swift current, the surges dash over the head of the unfortunate passenger. The capstan turns rapidly around, the raft is again moved under the ledge in smoother water, although the surges had almost claimed their victim—the unfortunate looses his lashing, stands erect and rests his limbs which had been stripped of their covering by the boiling current. When sufficiently recovered he again takes his seat and makes himself fast, again the capstan heaves, alas. the rope is again fast in the rocks and cannot be moved except up and down the stream, again the capstan turns, the raft is brought close to the perpendicular cliff with sufficient force to lift the the stern free from the water. The rapids dash over the bow of the raft and fall harmless in front of the sorrow-stricken. What shall now be done? The rope is still fast, the sun is fading in the western horizon and the sable mantle of night will soon veil the scene. Shall this man be left to spend another gloomy night in the arms of death? Another attempt must be made, again the lightning flashes to Buffalo—a boat wanted. A boat is furnished and the railroad agent promptly placed the same upon the cars. The engineer taxes the speed of his engine to its utmost capacity, as human life might depend upon the arrival of the cars, in the shortest possible time—the cars arrive—ere the speed of the cars is arrested, the crowd bear the boat upon their shoulders to the scene of peril— all with one thought, the rescue. So there is yet hope that the rescue may be accomplished before nightfall. Again another call is made for rope; another tackle block is found and stripped; the boat lowered into the stream, carefully the rope slides out from the capstan, until she reaches the fearful cliff, a surge strikes the boat, she almost poises over the cascade; the rope stretches but little and that little loses her over the cliff, and forces a plank from her side, the affrighted man has unloosed his lashings and is standing up—the boat strikes the raft—the concussion throws him off and he is seen tottering from time into eternity. A wail is heard from the lips of the thousands of anxious spectators; some run to the brink of the precipice to witness the last struggle. Ladies swoon and drop like soldiers on a battle field; the multitude heave a sigh and turn their faces homeward, few having tasted food since the dawn of day.

The following article was written to the Albany Register:

NIAGARA FALLS, July, 19, 1853.

It is verging toward midnight on the 18th of July, 1853, and the stars shine calmly down through a delicious atmosphere, upon the village of Niagara Falls. Music gives life to the joyous dance at the Cataract and the International Hotels, and pleasure seekers here, congregated from all parts of the continent, have found enjoyment. Many fair women and brave men still linger on Goat Island, unwilling to sever from scenes and sounds so full of harmony—so congenial to the pure activity of soul, which marks alike the worshiper of God and the being who sins lightly, if at all, by indulging in dreams of earthly love and honor. One plighted couple are returning, and have halted for a moment on the bridge, the hand of each clasped in each other's, as they look upward on the rapids. A thin cloud is drawn for a few moments over the resplendent stars, like the dropping of a bridal veil, and the shadow rests on the arrowy foam of the furious river. And they whisper of approaching union, and the years of happiness which they doubt not the good God has in store for them that love Him so. But what was that dark object which so suddenly sprung into view on the very verge of the horizon above them, as though swung heavenward by a huge wave? He says it was but a taller, shadowed pitch of the wild waters or a floating log. What shook the bridge then, and did you not hear a shreik, faint and smothered, as though it came from a cavern deep in the earth? Oh no! It was but the strong blow of a eddying whirl of the fierce river which made the bridge tremble a very little more than it usually trembles; and if you heard a cry, it was but the near shreik of some high-wheeling night bird. There can be no misery near us in a place, and at a time like this, where all is so calm but the great river exulting in its strength, and where we can almost see God's good angels, half unsphered, watching the world. The ganzy cloud floats westward, and the stars shine out in glory, and the lovers walk blissfully on and cross the bridge and Heaven blesses them in dreams that night, while the music of the joyous dancers below sounds in their visions a harmony of heaven.

But it was no dead tree trunk, nor single lifted, cloud shadowed wave, that caught for a single second that gentle maiden's eye. It was a boat and in it were two men—around each were twined loves as deep, if not so exalted and pure, as those which hallow and beautify her and her's. It was not a strong swirl of the wild waters that made the firm bridge tremble a little more than it always trembles in the strong current. It was the crashing, like an eggshell, of the strong-built boat when it dashed against the pier and whirled under the bridge in fragments. It was not the scream of a night-bird, whirling in the dusky air above her, which startled the soft-hearted maiden; but was the conjoined agonies of two strong-lunged, despairing men, which burst forth into a yell, which was all but drowned in the deep roar of the majestic river, and came as but in a whisper to the ear of the tender maiden, who was intently listening, scarce two hundred feet away. One of the strong men is carried downward, unseen save by God and the starry eyes of night. Fifteen hundred or two thousand feet are but as a step for the great torrent, though if they lived until they reached the verge of the fall, Heaven only knows how much misery was endured, or how surely hope eternal and well-founded sprung up in his soul, while the wrathful river took that step ere she dashed him on the pile of rocks one hundred and fifty feet below and broke forever the ligatures of hope and love that bound him to the world.

But for the second! Far better would it have been, in human judgment, had he too been swept away at once into eternity. But not so, for there are many lessons to be drawn from the troubled remnant of his life—at least by those who witnessed it.

About 500 feet below the bridge, and about one-third of the way across from the main shore, a log is embedded in the rapids. It lies in the direction of the torrent, and at the lower end, for a length of about fifteen feet rises above water, then seems to sink a little, like the hollow of a saddle, and is below water for a foot or two and then rises at an angle of about forty-five degrees for four or five feet and so ends abruptly. At about four o'clock in the morning the survivor, a lusty man of twenty summers or thereabouts, was discovered clinging to the upper part of the log, and at once the village was astir. It was a strange chance that threw him on this mere point—the only one between the bridge and fall where the foot of man could rest. It would seem that Providence, by so miraculous an interposition for his present safety, gave assurance for his final rescue. But God knows best, and the world would be a chaos were not the issue of our efforts by Him directed. We have only our duties before us and He will take care of results.

What fascination there is in the peril of another, though he be a stranger, and whatever may be his rank in life, his attainments or his qualities.

What a pity it is that the peril which so fascinates us, and nerves us up to deeds of heroism, and sacrifices of money, and property, and comfort, must, in the general, be an apparent peril of life or limb. Those slow and deadly dangers which besets our neighbors and ourselves, those parents of crime, which aims at the destruction of physical vigor and moral purity, which contaminate life in the fountain wither it in maturity, which create the drunkard, the libertine, the robber, and the murderer, alas! they fright but few of us, but we put not on our armor to battle against them unto the death.

I could hardly take my eyes from that poor man from the first time I saw him until his fate was decided. There were hundreds there, who would cheerfully imperiled their own lives, could reason have been cajoled into holding out the slightest hope of the risks contributing to the salvation of the stranger. Property was sacrificed without hesitation, for him, and one kind gentleman, a stranger, from—the Lord knows where, but may he be remembered in Heaven—offered a thousand dollars to save the stranger.

When I first saw him in the morning he was clinging to the log and occasionally raising his head above the top and looking from side to side. He must have realized fully the almost hopeless danger of his situation, and was sick at heart, as well as chilled by the night air, and the spray sapping his strength for so many slow ebbing hours. His head was bare, but otherwise he was fully clothed. It was impossible for the human voice to reach him. No voice of encouragement to reach him, but the sympathizing spirit of the people was not discouraged, and sought to uphold him by signs. He was a German and some kind person caused to be painted in big letters, in German, on canvas, the words, "WE WILL SAVE YOU," and nailed it, like a banner, on the front of a building on the bank. He saw and understood it, and waved his hands, in gratitude, we trust, in gratitude. The people, full of sympathy, thronged the shore, both island and bridge. Alas! they could do nothing, unless it were by their mere presence, to encourage hope and strengthen his sometimes failing courage.

It is painful to record the efforts that were made for his relief and extrication and yet a summary of them may not be devoid of interest. In doing so it is necessary to recall his position in the torrent. All above was a wild waste of water, rushing downward over curved ledges of rock crossing awthart the stream, and so was all below, save that the log to which he clung was imbedded in a basin of foaming water between two ledges, and the water there seemed less unquiet. From the ledges above the fall was more than a foot. On his left the great mass of the river came down in a tumult of green waves and eddies, on his right lay first the foaming basin, the strong current of a minor channel of the river, and then broken water and an eddy, at the foot of which was a small mass of rocks above water and blackened logs, from which access to a small wooded island below seemed easy. On that island he would be safe, for it could be reached, though with much difficulty, from Goat or Bath Island, in a boat. To cross the furious channel on his left to the main shore was impossible.

There he lay from the time he was discovered, until, I should think, about half-past four in the afternoon, the sun beating on his uncovered head, and without food. Attempts were made to lower food to him from the bridge, the food being enclosed at one time in a basket, and at least twice in air-tight tin cans, but all these attempts were unsuccessful. How he endured all he did seems strange to me. God had certainly given him a strong frame and a stout heart and he would have made a gallant sailor.

At nine o'clock the first attempt at rescue was made. No one had any confidence in it, but people were impatient to do something, though a message had been dispatched to Buffalo for a life-boat, which was expected on the next train. A strong light skiff was launched from Bath Island, drawn out into the stream, and let down by two ropes in the lesser channel. She filled and upset, however, and was lost.

But here comes the life-boat from Buffalo, and the crowd sent up a cheer which rises to Heaven, and even crosses to the poor man on the log, and he erects himself in expectation. It is borne across the bridge, and the gentleman having it in charge examines from different points on the bank and the bridge, the obstacles to be overcome. It is almost evident that they are insuperable, but there is a bare possibility of success, and that is sufficient. The boat is launched, and the bridge is cleared of all but the workers, and she is gradually lowered. What a beautiful boat she is, and how triumphantly she rides the wild swells! Now she passes down the main shute, and they begin to work her toward the log, while the man hangs with his hands on the top of it, his eyes devouring the space between himself, and what he trusts, is his preserver. And, indeed, there would seem scarce room to doubt that he was on the point of being rescued. But now the boat from the entangling of the rope in the rocks below, or from some other cause, upsets, and then she rises like a duck—and now she is just a little above the log, and in a second more the man will be safe. My God! she swings a little beyond, in a swift eddy, and does not right again. I shut my eyes, and when I open them again, she is far off in the broad channel by the main shore, held by a single rope and almost sunk by the weight and force of the current. The man, the poor man, who but just now was waving his hands this way and that way to guide the people in the management of the ropes, and who, I could swear, from the motion of his head, shouted with joy as the boat neared him, was now clasping the upright portion of the log. His head droops, and despair, I fear, is in his heart, and so he lies, inanimate on the thing he rests on, for fully an hour.

But the good people are not discouraged; they now commence building a raft. It is made of two long square timbers, with a platform firmly spiked on at one end, and occasional crosspieces to the other end, on which is lashed a barrel. While this is being done a crowd of men bring upon poles on their shoulders a large broad-beamed skiff. It is concluded to try this before the raft, and it is launched from Bath Island, let down the channel and worked across stream to the log. Thank God, the man is safe now! This boat has worked admirably, and he is safe! Alas! the rope has, somehow or other, got entangled with the log, and though her prow lies on the left and at the very stem of the log, she cannot be moved a foot. The man has been all attention, for some time. He crawls along the log and tries to move the boat. He cannot stir it. He crawls in and bales out some of the water with his hands, and then pushes the log. He gets upon the log and pushes the boat. Again he gets into the boat and bales with his hands. He then takes off both boots and bales with one of them. He puts on his boots and taking off his coat, folds it and lays it in the bow of the boat. He gets upon the log, and walks to the further end, lies down upon it, and thrusts his arm into the water. He gets the rope, and pulls with all his might, and then goes to the boat and pushes it. And so he works,—how long it seemed to me!—sometimes in one place and sometimes in the other, and continually in vain. How I longed for a voice to tell him to keep still, and to husband his strength, the whole of which might yet be requisite to save him. But now he despairs again. God does seem to have declared against him! But now, after a long interval, they are shooting the raft over the rail of the bridge. They have launched it and down it floats. Now it is in the swift current, and the barrel disappears in the overcharging foam. But it holds together nobly, and passes the shell, and is drawn safely to the log. The man, so long confined there, I am sure, gives a cheer. He sits down on the platform, and fixes his feet in and takes hold of stays and loops fixed to the floor of the raft, and they begin to haul on the ropes. This must have been between four and five o'clock. For a full hour, as it seemed to me, they endeavored to draw the raft directly up the stream, but to drag it up the first fall or ledge was impossible— but still they pulled with a will and now the raft fell back suddenly and swiftly; surely the ropes must have parted, and a perceptable shudder runs through the mass of men around me. So, too, thinks the man, for he stands upon his feet, and with a hurried glance around him, stands prepared to jump and swim for his life; but he is instantly reassured, and calmly resumes his seat, for they had merely slackened the ropes preparatory to trying to guide the raft to the right or island shore. They do guide it successfully— slowly, but steadily, it swims far away from the log, and the man sits there like a statue. He lies upon the raft with his head drooping, as though half slumbering, and then raises it with a start, like one contending with sleep or exhaustion. And now the raft is on the edge, in the raging torrent, the water arches over the barrel in front—the raft is pressed down—and he is waist deep. The waves force him backward and rush up to his mouth, and he will be drowned; but now, with a mighty effort, he bows forward with his head under water, draws out his feet and throws them backwards so that he is kneeling, holding on with his hands, and with head erect. Again the raft slides to the left, out of the swiftest water; and there she lies so long! What is the matter now? Alas! the rope has caught in a ledge of rock above and some new contrivance must be resorted to clear it. Again is hope deferred, yes, almost crushed.

But it is now nearly six o'clock, and the large ferry boat is put in the water, and, the inexperienced say, it must be easy to lay her alongside the raft. We can see hope rekindle in the bosom of the sufferer. Carefully the boat is let down and is nearly there. The boat almost touches the raft, and the man rises, ready to step in. But, my God! the force of the current dashes her against the raft, and he is thrown into the water! Strike out for your life! Cross but one rod of stormy water and you are safe! Alas! he swims but faintly, he despairs, and throws himself backward, and a dark spot is seen hurrying toward the fall. As he reaches the verge, with a spasmodic effort he raises breast high from the water, and the poor sufferer, whom we have watched so long, will be seen no more on earth. He has joined his companion, and may Heaven have mercy upon them.

This melancholy affair may be summed up in a few words: If the unfortunate man had not loosened his fastenings to the raft on the approach of the boat, and if his strength had been sufficient to endure the fatigue of another ten hours on the raft, (as nothing could be done for him in the darkness of the night,) in all probability he might have been brought to Chapin's Island the following day, from which his rescue would have been comparatively easy.

The body of the unfortunate Hanniman was found on the following Saturday, July 23rd, near Suspension Bridge, and decently interred by Mr. Sternes, the town poor master. The body of Avery was never recovered.

Pierce's Novel Brigade.

At the junction of the Portage Road with Main Street in this city, there was a public house for many years, which, during the War of 1812, was kept by a man named Gad Pierce, who was an active frontier partisan. When hostilities commenced between the two countries, there was a very small number of troops on the American side of the river, and only a single company to garrison Fort Niagara. It was expected, every night, that the Fort would be attacked by the British, who had a large force of men at Fort George. Mr. Pierce, aware of this state of affairs, one day raised all the inhabitants in the surrounding country, and had them assemble at Lewiston. Horses of every kind were brought into requisition, and, when the citizens were mounted, they appeared at a distance like a formidable troop of cavalry. Among them, too, were several of the Tuscarora Indians, who entered with spirit into the manouver. Instead of swords, they used walking canes, sticks and ramrods. Several of the ramrods were of polished steel or iron, which made a very bright and flashy appearance. The cavalcade moved from Lewiston, along the river road, in sight of the enemy, and entered Fort Niagara. The blankets of the Indians fluttering in the wind, the various habiliments of the farmers, the limping and over-strained plow horse, the nibbling gait and twitching head of the wild pony, with now and then a noble looking horse, formed, to those who were near, a most ludicrous spectacle. In the fort, they dismounted, and performed some slight evolutions in a most laughable manner. At the command to mount, some of the Indians executed the order in such a masterly way as to throw themselves entirely over their ponies. To the British, the imposing appearance of the troops with their steel ramrods, which glittered in the sun like broadswords, had the desired effect: the contemplated attack was not made.

At the time of the general invasion of the frontier, Mr. Pierce had his family removed to a place of safety, but would not himself quit the premises. He and four others formed the little garrison, with which he determined to defend his home. They waited for the approach of the enemy. At length a company of British regulars appeared and a fire was opened upon them. They continued the defence for some time, but, as their opponents were numerous, it was impossible to keep them at a distance. A part advanced upon the front of the house, and succeeded in breaking down the door, firing their guns as they entered. The defenders effected their escape in an opposite direction without any of their number being wounded. Whether the attacking party suffered any loss was not known.

An Indian Adventure.

Just below the mountain and to the right of the road which descends from the Tuscarora village, there lived a man by the name of Sparrow Sage, who was driven away from his home, on the 19th of December, 1813, during the invasion of the Niagara Frontier by the British. But, for the purpose of securing his harvest, he and his wife returned the following summer to their exposed and solitary dwelling. One day, while Mr. Sage was at work in a field some distance from the house, an Indian, attached to the British cause, entered the house and demanded something to eat, speaking in broken English. Mrs. Sage, being entirely alone, immediately obeyed his bidding, in hopes that after eating he would go away. But in this she was disappointed.

for as soon as he had finished his repast he informed her that he lived at Grand River, Canada, and that he had come after her to go with him as his squaw. She replied that it could not be, as she already had a husband. "No! no!" he angrily exclaimed, "you very pretty; you must be my squaw; you shall go." In vain she told him that her husband and others were near by and that he had better go way or else he might get killed. The Indian then took down Mr. Sage's gun and, finding it unloaded, put it back again, He then ransacked the house, commanding Mrs. Sage not to leave his sight, at the same time keeping his eyes upon her. He took as much as he could carry of such things as he mostly desired, and, seizing Mrs. Sage forcibly by the arm, he dragged her out of the back door, and thence towards the woods, in the direction of Fort Niagara, at that time occupied by the British. The husband hearing the screams of his wife, hurried towards the house, seized an ax which was lying at the door, and followed in pursuit. He came up to them at a fence, on the border of the forest. Not letting go his hold, the savage fired at Mr. Sage as he ran towards them. But, luckily, the ball did not take effect, and just as the Indian was raising his victim to throw her over the fence, a blow from the ax broke his rifle and made him let go of Mrs. Sage. Hastily consulting his own safety, he leaped over the fence, but while doing so he received another blow from the ax. The forest resounded with his yells, as he made off with all possible speed into the thick woods. Mr. Sage did not think it proper to pursue, but returning with his wife, they immediately left their dangerous habitation for a place of safety.

Mr. William Molyneaux, the father of Mrs. Sage, had occupied the same residence the winter before, but he and his family were also compelled to flee to a place of safety. About a month after he returned, and, upon entering the house, he found two dead Indians lying upon the floor. A party of American soldiers had come upon them unexpectedly, while they were carousing upon the good fare which the occupants had left. They were, no doubt, abroad for murder and destruction, and met the fate which they intended for others. Mr. Molyneaux dragged their bodies from the house, and as he had no aid nor time to bury them, he formed around them a large pile of logs and rails, and, setting fire to it, they were consumed. The British Indians considered it quite an affront, and threatened vengeance, but it was an empty threat, as they had already done all the harm they could.

A Narrow Escape.

It was in the early morning, on the 19th of December, 1813, the weather being cold, and the bleak winds howling, when the inhabitants of Lewiston were aroused from their quiet slumbers and compelled to leave their comfortable homes and flee from a cruel and relentless foe, who had just crossed the river, and was spreading death and desolation all along the border. The roads had been badly broken up, and were frozen in a state that it was impossible to proceed with wagons, and, there being little snow, only slow progress could be made with sleighs. In the rear of the fugitives, who were hastening with all possible speed along the Ridge Road, was a two-horse sleigh, driven by a young man who walked beside his horses. In the sleigh lay his brother, who one week before had his leg amputated just below the knee. He was in a very feeble condition, and to proceed rapidly, rough as the roads then were, would have been death to him.

Although the enemy was not far in the rear, there was no alternative but to continue the moderate pace at which they were moving. The driver, who was armed with a trusty rifle, would frequently cast anxious glances behind him, knowing that the enemy was not far in the rear. At length the war-whoop of the British Indians, with its accompanying yells, broke upon his ears. The disabled brother besought the other to leave him to his fate and flee for his life. "No," he replied, "if we are to die, we will perish together." The party of Indians that pursued them was in full sight and one, far in advance of the others, called upon them to stop, making threatening gestures, and raising his rifle as if to shoot.

With the same slow pace the horses proceeded, and the driver was coolly collecting himself for the conflict, in which such fearful odds were against him. The Indian sprang forward and was within a few paces of the sleigh, when the young man, suddenly turning himself, quickly raised his rifle and fired upon his pursuer, who fell forward a corpse, his body rolling out of the road. A yell of vengeance, from the band in the rear, came like a knell of death upon the ears of the brothers. At that moment a band of friendly Tuscaroras were seen descending the adjacent hill, and the well directed fire which they opened on the British Indians, obliged the latter to hastily retire.

The driver of the sleigh was the late Hon. Bates Cook, and the invalid was the late Lathrop Cook, names that have been familiar household words for many years.

Capt. Webb's Last Swim.

Capt. Matthew Webb, the famous English swimmer, made the attempt to swim through the Rapids and Whirlpool of Niagara River on the afternoon of July 24th, 1883, and lost his life in the effort. As he had publicly announced he would do, Capt. Webb left the Clifton House, on the Canada side, at 4 o'clock, and proceeded down the bank to the ferry landing. Here he stepped into a small boat manned by Jack McCloy, ferryman, and was rowed down the river to opposite the old Pleasure Grounds, just above the old Maid of the Mist landing. At 4.25 he jumped from the boat into the river. A moment later he rose gracefully to the surface and, swimming with infinite ease and power, struck boldly out. He cleared the water with strong and steady strokes, swimming on his breast with his head clear from the surface. He kept in the centre of the stream and the strong eddies which occasionally swirled past him seemed in no way to impede or swerve him from his course. As he approached the Railway Suspension Bridge, which he passed at 5.33, the flow of the current increased with remarkable rapidity. There were about two hundred spectators on the bridge who saw the intrepid swimmer glide towards them, pass beneath them, and ere they could reach the north side of the structure, he was fifty yards down the current. He was carried along as fast as the eye could follow him. With speechless wonder and fear he was seen to reach the first furious billows of the rapids. Onward he sped like a feather in the sea. High on the crest of a huge billow his head and shoulders gleamed for an instant and then he was lost in a dark abyss of turmoiling water. Again he appeared, his arms steadily moving as if balancing himself for a plunge into another mighty wave. The tumbling, rushing, swirling element seemed to give forth an angry, sullen roar as if sounding the death knell of the ill-fated swimmer. Once more away down the Rapids he was seen still apparently braving fate and stemming the seething waters with marvelous skill and endurance. Instead of being whirled hither and thither as might have been expected he was carried with furious rapidity onward almost in a straight course.

For nearly a mile he was hurried forward by the tumultuous rushing waters and still he seemed to be riding the awful billows in safety. In two minutes after he had passed under the Suspension Bridge he had been hurried through the terrible Rapids and arrived at the mouth of the great Whirlpool. Reaching what seemed to be less troubled and dangerous waters, it was said by some, that he raised his head well above the surface, gazed for an instant towards the American side and then turned his face to the high bluff on the Canadian side. A second later he dived or sank and was seen no more. But Mr. Culhane, of the Canadian customs force, who was at the inclined railway near the Whirpool, when Webb came down the river, with a couple of boys and some ladies, says that he and his party saw Webb distinctly for a minute before he reached the Whirlpool, and they were confident that he was either dead or insensible prior to that time. As the body approached the Whirlpool, the head seemed to be hanging to one side, and the body appeared to have no life in it. Once it raised a little out of the water by an extra eddy, but fell back as if lifeless. He believes that Webb had endurance enough to swim a long distance, but was buffetted to death by the pressure of tons upon tons of water in the Rapids. Therefore he must have been killed or rendered insensible ere he got to the Whirlpool, into which he was without doubt drawn. The rapidity of the current that carried Webb to his doom may be gathered from the fact that it only took two minutes to carry him from the bridge to the Whirpool fully three-fourths of a mile distant. Notwithstanding the fact that Webb's fatal swim was witnessed by a large number of people, much doubt was expressed as to whether he might not have left the river alive at some point beyond the observation of the spectators. All uncertainty on these points were, however, removed by the finding of Capt. Webb's body about noon on Saturday, July 28, 1883, four days after his disappearance, by Richard W. Turner, of Youngstown, about a mile and a half below, Lewiston. Capt. Matthew Webb was a native of England and 35 years of age. His father lives in Shropshier, England, and there were 13 children in the family, eight being boys. He learned to swim when eight years old, being encouraged in his ventures by his father. While yet a mere youth, he ran away to sea, and during his career before the mast became famous for his swimming feats, several of which were performed in saving human life. In 1872, while in South Africa, he won his first laurels as a public swimmer, and in a year following received a purse of $500 from the passengers of the steamer Russia and a medal from the humane society of London for saving the life of a sailor who was washed overboard. The achievement that gave him international fame was swimming the English channel naked and without aid of any kind, on which occasion he was in the water from 1 P. M. to 11 A. M. the next day. When he was dragged out of the water at the close of this exploit he was presented with $25,000 by the Prince of Wales. On one occasion he swam from Sandy Hook to Manhatten Beach during a storm that drove vessels into the harbor. In July, 1882, he beat Wade at Coney Island for the American championship and at different times has performed wonderful feats in the water, of which no record has been made. He made his home in Boston, where his wife, also of English birth and but a few years a resident in America, and two children were at the time of his untimely death. Never were physical prowess and courage worse applied than in the brave fellow's last adventure, which, even if successful, would have been of no pratical service to the world. Captain Webb seemed to have realized the danger of his undertaking, for in an interview he is reported to have said: "The current, they say, runs thirty miles an hour, and the river is ninety-five feet deep. It is wide just below the fall and narrows at the rapids. I am only afraid of the two awful ledges of rocks which jut out from the shores into the Whirlpool. The water fairly shrieks and hisses as it boils over them. Now, I want to avoid the sides, and yet I dare not go in the middle, for there lies the vortex, and that means death. I will go out into the river in a small boat just above the Suspension Bridge. The only clothing I shall wear will be the silk trunks I had on when I swam the English channel. At the time appointted I will leap into the river and float into the rapids. Of course I will make no attempt to go forward, for the fearful speed of the water will carry me through. When the water gets bad I will go under the surface and remain beneath until I am compelled to come up for breath. That will be pretty often, I'll wager. When I strike the Whirlpool I will strike out with all my strength, and try and keep away from the suckhole in the centre. I will begin with breast strokes and then use overhand strokes. My life will then depend upon my mucles and my breath, with a little touch of science behind them. It may take me two or three hours to get out of the Whirlpool which is about a quarter of a mile long. When I do get through I will try and land on the Canadian side, but if the current is too strong and swift, as I think it is, I will keep on down to Lewiston on the American side." Captain Webb's body now lies in Oakwood Cemetery at Niagara Falls, N. Y., near the grave of Francis Abbott, where it was buried July 31st, 1883, in the presence of his wife and numerous spectators, a small but beautiful monument marking his last resting place.

The "Old" Suspension Bridge.

As this was the first Railway Suspension Bridge that was ever built in the world, a brief history of its construction can not fail to be of some interest to the reading public.

For many years the barrier which the Niagara River chasm at this point, two miles below the falls, placed between Canada and the States had been regarded as an obstacle which should be surmounted, and on April 23, 1846, the present Suspension Bridge Co. received its American charter, and on June 9th, of the same year, it received its Canadian charter. In 1847 the company organized with the following directors:

American Directors—Wash. Hunt, Lot Clark, Samuel DeVeaux, George Field, L. Spaulding, I. C. Colton, and Charles Evans.

Canadian Directors—W. H. Merritt, Thomas C. Street, James Cunningham, Charles B. Stewart, James Oswald, Samuel Zimmerman and William O. Buchannan.

The work on the bridge was commenced in February, 1848, by Charles Elliet, Jr. The first connection between the two cliffs was made by a boy named Homan Walsh flying a kite, for which he received five dollars, across and thereby spanning the gorge with a small string. Later a cord was drawn over, next a rope, and so on until one of sufficient strength had been secured to draw over an iron cable of 36 strands No. 10 wire. Two small wooden towers having been erected one on each bank, the wire cable, 1160 feet long, was hauled across the chasm, and on the 13th of March, 1848, Mr. Elliet and others crossed in an iron basket suspended from the cable.

This basket was made and designed by Judge T. G. Hulett of this city to aid in the construction of the suspension bridge across the gorge. This basket was made of strips of band iron from one inch to one and one-half inches in width and fastened with rivets. At either end it was considerably higher than in the center. There was a seat at either end, their depth being about two feet. The manner in which its shape was decided upon is interesting. Judge Hulett and General Elliet first met at the old Eagle Tavern in December, 1847, during the time Thomas W. Fanning was proprietor. In the course of a conversation upon the great work that General Elliet had the contract for, the question of establishing communication between the banks by means of a cable and basket was discussed and recognized as possible.

The question then arose whether the basket should be of wood or iron. The first named material was the choice of Elliet, while Judge Hulett favored the latter. The matter of weight was an important fact, and in calculations which followed upon the plans of both men it was found that a basket constructed from Judge Hulett's plan would be 10 pounds lighter than one of wood, and it was adopted. The form of the basket was quickly decided by Judge Hulett and General Elliett arising from the rocking chairs in which they had been sitting and drawing them together, "there is the form of the basket," said Judge Hulett. The basket proved a source of considerable revenue, as the charge for transportation over and back was $1 for each person, and some days as high as $125 were taken.

The basket is now in the possession of the Buffalo Historical Society.

A foot-bridge, three feet in width, was soon constructed, and over this a great number of perons passed daily, each paying 25 cents to the contractor. A similar foot-bridge was now formed parallel to this, and the basket cable in the middle.

A terrific scene occurred just about this time. While the workmen were engaged on the second foot-bridge, which was constructed about 250 feet from the American shore, and about 150 feet from the British side, a tornado from the southwest, struck it, turning it quite over. Six men were at work on the flooring of the bridge at this awful moment, two of whom in a most unaccountable manner made their way to the shore upon fragments of boards. The unfinished structure ~~ ~n and w~ ed backwards and forw... like the ~~ ~n web of a spider, and f... ~at ~~~ man beings. 200 feet !... ~' supported by two strap.:~ ~.' were in constant expect~~ long plunge into the ra; who can fathom those just then? But the tin. held them to existence enough to outlast t~ the first cessation of the s~ a brave fellow workman ma~. iron basket, and with a ladder pro~. l-ed among the pelting of the furious rain to save the sufferers. He reached the wreck, placed his ladder in communication with it and the basket thus affording a means by which all were brought back safe to terra firma, uninjured in person, but well nigh scared to death.

On the 26th of July following, Mr. Elliet drove a span of horses and a heavy carraige over and back, accompanied by his lady.

This was the first bridge built across Niagara River and was completed in 1848. In 1853 the present railroad bridge was commenced and it was completed in the spring of 1855. The first railway train passed over it March 23rd, 1855.

The building of a suspension bridge for the purposes for which this one is used, was considered an experiment when it was projected, and many well known engineers predicted its failure. Its founders, however, had faith in its able engineer, John A. Roebling, who superintended its building and carried it to completion.

The cost of the first wagon bridge was about $60,000; that of the railway structure about $450,000.

Many improvements have been made within the past few years which have added a large additional expense. All of the woodwork, except the floor, has been removed and replaced by iron. The massive stone towers have given way to steel, so that the bridge was greatly beautified as well as strengthened by the change.

This is perhaps the strongest bridge of its kind in the world, and not only does it present a good view of the falls, but also of the rapids below the bridge. Under the superintendance of Mr. Thomas Reynolds this bridge is so well taken care of that a person feels as safe on it as he would on the solid ground. The following are the dimensions of the railway bridge:

Length of span from center to center of towers.......................... 822 feet.
Height of tower above rock on American Shore.................... 88 "

Height of tower above rock on Canadian Shore	78 feet.
Height of tower above floor of railway	60 "
Height of track above water	258 "
Number of wire cables	4
Diameter of each cable	10½ in.
No. of No. 9 wires in each cable	3,659
Ultimate aggregate strength of cables	12,400 tons.
Weight of superstructure	800 "
Weight of superstructure and maximum loads	1,250 "
Maximum weight cables and stays will support	7,309 "

On the 10th of October, 1854, during the construction of the railway bridge, a scaffold, upon which four men were at work, gave way, precipitating two of them into the gorge below, who struck the rocks and rolled into the river, while two caught onto the cables. From this place they were rescued by William Ellis, who bravely offered his services when volunteers were called for to go to their rescue, and for which service he received $25.

The fare for foot passengers is 10 cents over and back if returning the same day.

———♦———

Cantilever Bridge.

About 300 feet above the old suspension bridge is the great cantilever bridge. This is a double track railroad bridge designed to connect the New York Central and Michigan Central Railroads. The designs of this structure were worked out jointly by C. C. Schneider, chief engineer in charge of the work, and Edward Hayes, engineer of the Central Bridge Works.

The structure consists of two immense steel towers, 139 feet 6½ inches high, resting on stone piers 39 feet high. Each of these towers supports a cantilever 595 feet 5¾ inches long. The shore ends of the cantilevers are anchored to the abutment masonry or anchorage piers, and both river arms are connected by an intermediate span of 120 feet which is suspended from the extreme ends of the river arms.

The total length of the bridge proper is 910 feet 4⅜ inches between the centers of the anchorage piers; the clear span between towers being 470 feet. The height from the surface of the water to base of rail is 239 feet.

The first engine that ever passed over this bridge was the pony engine of Superintendent Burrows. They entered upon the bridge precisely at 11.43 on the 6th day of December, 1883, and moved forward quite slowly, and were two minutes in crossing the bridge proper. Running close to the edge on the Canadian shore, where a stop of some five minutes was made, when the party returned to this side in quicker time. The final test was made on the 20th day of the same month, when 20 heavy engines and 40 loaded cars were run upon the bridge at once.

New Suspension Bridge.

About one-eighth of a mile below the falls is a carriage and foot bridge, built by American and Canadian capitalists. This bridge was built of iron and wood and was completed in 1868, and was opened for traffic Jan. 2, 1869. This bridge stood the brunt of some terrible gales in safety for a number of years. It was afterwards remodeled and became practically new. New steel towers, anchor pits, iron girders, needle beams, suspenders, guys, a widened wooden road-way, iron railings and other improvements that made it more than ever, as it was believed, thoroughly proof against any assault of the elements. But hardly had it been completed before the destroyer came.

What proved to be a most disastrous gale began to show its teeth on the afternoon of the ninth of January 1889, and gradually increased its force until it gained during the night a velocity of about 100 miles an hour. Trees, fences, outbuildings and numerous other things readily succumbed to this terrific gale, and finally this beautiful structure itself yielded to the force of the wind and dropped into the gorge below.

The bridge must have fallen about 3 o'clock on the morning of the 10th. None of the bridge or customs officials knew just when it fell, and it was not until after daylight that the full disaster became known. The steel towers, the four great cables, the anchorages and a lot of suspenders were still in place. Sections of the roadway lay at the bottom of the banks on either side of the river, but by far the larger portion had dropped into the river and sank to the bottom.

Although no eye saw the disaster, yet, at least, two men crossed the bridge just before the bridge went down. Dr. J. W. Hodge, who had been called to Canada about 10 o'clock, and on his return to the American side about midnight, received such an experience that he never will forget. He said that it was almost impossible to make his way across. The movement of the bridge was indicative of broken stays, and as it rose and fell in undulating swells and then seemed to drop bodily many feet, and the Doctor thought the roadway would certainly break from the cables. It is said that a man crossed over to Canada, yet later, and had to creep over on his hands and knees.

The length of this bridge, from shore to shore, is 1268 ft. The length of cables between anchorages is 1828 feet. The height of bridge above the water, is 190 feet. Its towers are 100 feet high.

While the bridge was being rebuilt the following fatal accident occurred: About nine o'clock on the morning of the 18th of April, 1889, an Italian named James Mundi started from the Canadian end with a box of bolts for workmen some distance out. He carried the box on his shoulder, distributing as he went, but when he got some distance from the Canadian shore he lost his balance and fell into the river below, a distance of 175 feet. Strangely enough the fall did not kill him, though one arm was seen to be useless, he struck out for the shore. Planks were thrown from the bridge for his assistance, but proved of no avail. A boat started for him but before it could reach him the poor fellow sank and was seen no more.

---◆---

Lewiston Bridge.

The Lewiston bridge was commenced in 1849, and finished in 1850. Capt. Edward Sorrell was its chief engineer and Thomas M. Griffith assistant engineer. The total length of cables was 1,245 feet and distance between the towers 1,040 feet. The bridge was supported by 10 cables, five on each side, and the strength of the bridge was estimated at about 835 tons. It had a roadway 20 feet wide, giving ample room for teams to pass and also for a footway. It was blown down by a wind storm on April 16th, 1864, under peculiar circumstances. Some time previous there occurred a big ice jam, and the ice rose high enough to fasten onto the guys and those in charge of the structure fearing that when the ice went out it would carry the bridge with it, the guys were taken up on the bridge. The ice passed out without doing any injury and there was a week or more of good weather during which the bridge was used as usual. But the bridge superintendent neglected to replace the guys and the wind carried it away as above stated. There were two persons on the bridge when the wind began to sway it previons to its fall, but they escaped without injury. The capital stock was $60,000— $30,000 American and $30,000 Canadian —but the American side cost the most owing to the towers being somewhat higher and were built of Lockport cut stone. The Canadian towers were built of stone from the Queenston quarries nearby and were less expensive. The old company sold out its franchise, bridge, land and approaches thereto to Theodore Irwin of Oswego, Sam Sloan of New York, and their associates, the directors of the R., W. & O. No effort was ever made to rebuild the structure and the cables and other parts of the wreck hang suspended over the river to this day. An old report says that some years ago a desperate criminal climbed over the cables hanging over the river, and escaped into Canada from officers who were in pursuit. A short time ago a young man attempted to give an exhibition in walking across and fell into the water. He escaped with a ducking.

Maid of the Mist.

The Maid of the Mist was a staunch little steamer of about 110 tons burden, built in 1854, (the first Maid of the Mist was built in 1846) and was employed in carrying pleasure parties from her landing, which was a little above the Railway Suspension Bridge, to the falls and back. It being employed in this capacity for a number of years, her owner conceived the idea of running her through the rapids for the purpose of getting her clear of a certain mortgage to which she was subject while in the locality she then was. For this purpose he engaged two sailors who were used to running the rapids in the St. Lawrence river, but when the day came for them to run down the Niagara their courage failed them and they refused to go, so Mr. Joel R. Robinson was appealed to and he agreed to act as pilot for this fearful voyage. Mr. Jones, the engineer, consented to go with him, and Mr. McIntyre, a machinist, volunteered his services.

About three o'clock in the afternoon on the sixth day of June, 1861, these three men went on board of the boat. Jones took his place in the hold and McIntyre joined Robinson in the wheel house, Robinson took his place at the wheel. Self-possed and calm, he pulled the bell which was the signal anxiously waited for by the engineer, which was to start them on their perilous journey. With a shreik from her whistle and the sound of escaping steam she started up the stream for a little ways, then turning she took her course down the river. Many who saw her thought that the courage of the intrepid Robinson would fail and that he would turn again before reaching the rapids below the bridge, but on she rushed like a thing of life with her crew of brave hearts, and shot like an arrow, as many supposed into the very jaws of death. When about a third of the way down to the Whirlpool Rapids she was engulfed beneath the mighty waters, her smokestack was carried away and part of her deck stove in, Mr. Robinson was thrown flat on his back and Mr. McIntyre was thrown against the wheel house with such force as to break it through, while Jones went down on his knees before the glowing furnace, and, as he afterwards said, a more earnest prayer never was uttered. To that prayer he attributes their salvation from a watery grave. But emerging from her fearful baptism she rushed on at the mercy of the waves until she reached the smooth water in the Whirlpool on the American side where for the first time since entering this tremendous current Mr. Robinson again got her under his control. Taking a short turn to the right she again struck for the middle of the river to battle with the mighty waves. Startling the denizens of the neighboring banks by the shrieks of her whistle and fighting her way through the rapids passing the Devil's Hole, she entered the more placid water at Lewiston, a triumphant conqueror, in $17\frac{1}{2}$ minutes from the time she passed under the railway suspension bridge.

Thus was performed one of the most daring feats on record, and many persons enquire how it was possible for them to get through these tremendous waters without getting lost. The answer invariably is: "I don't know."

This can not be called a foolhardy feat, for Mr. Robinson was a very cool and heroic man. He had at various times navigated the rapids above the falls, when it was necessary for him to do so for the purpose of saving life; and he had full confidence in himself that he could guide the little "Maid" through this river of breakers and land her safely in the smooth waters below.

But he found the water rougher than he had anticipated. And to the public eye it was simply luck and chance that the voyage terminated so fortunately. As an instance of the coolness of Mr. Robinson during this hasty trip, we would simply say, that, when Mr McIntyre was thrown against the wheel house, for some reason or other he was unable to arise, so Mr. Robinson put his foot gently on his breast to keep him from rolling to and fro and thus held him until the end of the journey. This trip had a decided effect upon Mr. Robinson, and some attribute his death to this cause, but this is not true, for the disease which terminated his life was contracted at New Orleans some time after.

Joel R. Robinson.

Joel R. Robinson was born in Springfield, Mass., on the 27th day of September, 1808, and at an early date came to Niagara Falls, which place he made his home until his death. As a navigator of the rapids he had no equal, and whenever it became necessary to rescue a human being from the jaws of those fearful waters, Robinson was always ready to render all the aid in his power.

In the summer of 1838, while some repairs were being made on the bridge leading from the main shore to Bath Island, a man by the name of Chapin fell from the bridge and lodged on a small island below. This island which is hardly more than 30 feet square is covered with a few evergreen trees and bears his name, who, in all probability, was its first occupant. All eyes were turned on Robinson, as the only one who could rescue the man from his perilous position. Robinson launched his boat from the foot of Bath Island, picking his way skillfully and cautiously through the rapids to the little island, took Chapin and brought him safely to shore.

The next instance we have of saving life we copy from the work of G. W. Hawley:. "In the summer of 1841, a Mr. Allen started for Chippawa in a boat, just before sunset. Being anxious to get across before dark, he applied his oars with such vigor that one of them was broken when he was about opposite the middle Sister. With the remaining oar he tried to reach the head of Goat Island. The current, however, set too strongly towards the great Canadian Rapids and his only hope was to reach the outer Sister. Nearing this and not being able to run his boat on it, he sprang out, and, being a good swimmer, by a vigorous effort succeeded in getting on it. Certain of having a lonely, if not a quite unpleasant night, and being the fortunate possessor of two stray matches, he lighted a fire and solaced himself with his thoughts and his pipe. Next morning, taking off his red flannel shirt, he raised a signal of distress. Towards noon the unusual smoke and red flag attracted attention. The situation was soon ascertained and Robinson informed of it. Not long after a little red skiff was carried across Goat Island and launched in the channel just below Moss Islands. Robinson then pulled himself across to the middle Sister and tried in vain to find a point where he could cross to the outer one. Approaching darkness compelled him to suspend operations. He rowed back to Goat Island, procured some refreshments, returned to the middle Sister, threw them across to Allen and then left him to his second night's solitude. The next day Robinson took with him two long, light, but strong cords, with a properly shaped piece of lead weighing about a pound. Tying the lead to one of the lines he threw it across to Allen. He then fastened the other end of Allen's line to the bow of the skiff; and attaching his own cord to the boat also, he shoved it off. Allen drew it to himself, got into it, pushed off, and Robinson drew him to where he stood on the middle island. Then seating Allen in the stern of the skiff he returned across the rapids to Goat Island, where both were assisted up the bank by the spectators, and the little craft, too, which seemed almost as much of a hero and as great a favorite with the crowd as Robinson himself."

This was the second individual rescued by Robinson from islands which had been considered totally inaccessible. It is no exaggeration to say that there was not another man on the globe that could have saved Chapin and Allen as he did. His laurels as "Navigator of the Rapids" can never fade or decay. They are made perenial by the generous motives and humane acts through which they were won.

Joel R. Robinson died June 30, 1863.

www.ingramcontent.com/pod-product-compliance
Lightning Source LLC
Chambersburg PA
CBHW020106170426
43199CB00009B/414